CREED

CREED

*Daily devotionals for each
day of the year*

By Rusty Budde

Xulon Press

Xulon Press
2301 Lucien Way #415
Maitland, FL 32751
407.339.4217
www.xulonpress.com

Unless otherwise indicated, Scripture quotations taken from the New King James Version (NKJV). Copyright © 1982 by Thomas Nelson, Inc. Used by permission. All rights reserved.

Printed in the United States of America.

ISBN-13: 978-1-6305-0310-9

This book is dedicated to my beautiful daughter
and granddaughter Amanda Lee and Kamala Lee.

Special thanks to
Cheryl Jones Bamonte

Special thanks to all the prayer warriors
who stay constant in Love for our Lord.

TODAY'S PERSONAL MESSAGE
Opening Prayer

Good morning Jesus. I want to thank you
For the good night's sleep.
I am a happy man since you came into my Life.
Thank you for blessing me with all your healing power
you have in store for me today. I praise you Father God
for all that you do in my Life.
God bless all my friends and family.
I love you Jesus today tomorrow
And forever.
Amen Amen Amen.

Rusty Budde 11.3.2017

Today's Personal Message
January 1st

My prayer for you today is to find God's teachable
spirit inside yourself, search for the path that God
has planned for you, and know that with Him
all things are possible.
May God bless you all and have a Happy New Year!

"Come to me, all you who are weary and
burdened, and I will give you rest."
Matthew 11:28

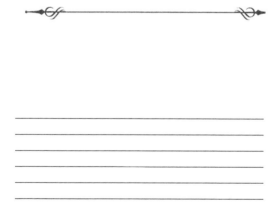

_____
_____
_____
_____
_____
_____

Today's Personal Message
January 2nd

*My Prayer for you today is to relax, close your eyes
and spend precious time in the presence of God.
For it pleases Him.
God bless you all.*

*"And my God will meet all your needs according to his
glorious riches in Christ Jesus."*
Philippians 4:19

Today's Personal Message

January 3rd

My prayer for you today is that you are not
weighed down by everyday problems but lifted up
into His Glorious Light.
May God bless us all.

"The Lord is good, a strong hold in the day of trouble;
and he knoweth them that trust in him."
Nahum 1:7

_____
_____
_____
_____
_____
_____

Today's Personal Message

January 4th

My prayer for you today is that you learn to trust Jesus.
He will take you places you have never dreamed of.
May God our Father bless you and all who hear his voice.

"And we know that all things work together
for good to them that love God, to them who
are the called according to his purpose."
Romans 8:28

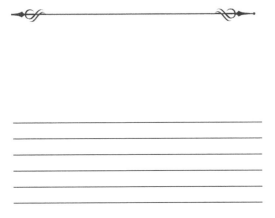

_____
_____
_____
_____
_____
_____

TODAY'S PERSONAL MESSAGE
January 5th

My prayer for you today is to find your faith in Jesus!
Depend on Him for strength and guidance every step of
the way; learn to know God's Love for you, staying on the
path He has set before you, the truth lies just ahead.
God bless you all.

"Look to the Lord and his strength;
seek his face always"
Psalm 105:4

_____
_____
_____
_____
_____
_____

Today's Personal Message
January 6th

My prayer for you today is to learn to trust God's will, for there is no limit to what He can and will do for you. Prepare yourselves for the amazing gifts to come.
God bless you all.

"Give thanks to the Lord, for he is good; his love endures forever."
Psalm 118:1

TODAY'S PERSONAL MESSAGE
January 7th

My prayer for you today is that you draw near to God closer and closer praising His Name every day giving thanks for all He does for you. May God bless us all.

"Be strong and courageous. Do not be afraid or terrified because of them, for the Lord your God goes with you; he shall never leave you nor forsake you."
Deuteronomy 31:6

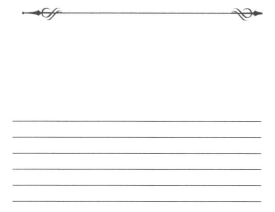

_____
_____
_____
_____
_____
_____

TODAY'S PERSONAL MESSAGE
January 8th

*My prayer for you today is that you learn to
live by faith, Joy and hope, and stay constantly
faithful in prayer. Amen
May God bless us all.*

*"Give thanks in all circumstances, for this is
God's will for you in Christ Jesus."
Thessalonians 5:18*

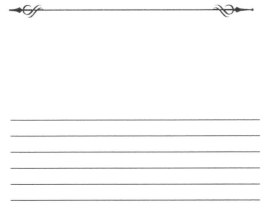

_____
_____
_____
_____
_____
_____

TODAY'S PERSONAL MESSAGE
January 9th

*My prayer for you today is that you slow down
and enjoy your journey with Jesus by your side.
May God our Father guide and bless your day.*

*"I have told you these things, so that
In me you may have peace. In this world
You will have trouble. But take heart!
I have overcome the world."*
John 16:33

_____
_____
_____
_____
_____
_____

TODAY'S PERSONAL MESSAGE
January 10th

*My prayer for you today is to receive the
Healing Peace that God our Father has stored up
For you and believe and receive your miracle.
God bless you and keep you in His arms!*

*Then Jesus said, "Did I not tell you that if you
Believed, you would see the glory of God."
John 11:40*

TODAY'S PERSONAL MESSAGE
January 11th

My prayer for you today is that you let go
And trust in God's awesome power. May God
Bless each of you today and every day of your life.

"But store up for yourselves treasures in heaven,
Where moth and rust do not destroy, and where thieves
do not break in and steal. For where your treasure is,
there your heart will be also."
Matthew 6:20-21

TODAY'S PERSONAL MESSAGE
January 12th

*My prayer for you today is to know that God is with you at
all times, giving you strength to find your way
in this crazy world, hold him close to you and let him lead
you to paradise. Amen! Pray for each other.
God bless you all.*

"Blessed are all who take refuge in Him."
Psalm 2:12

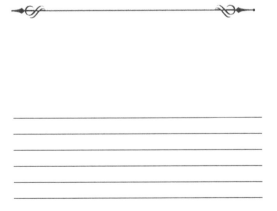

_____

_____

_____

_____

_____

_____

Today's Personal Message

January 13th

My prayer for you today is that you be willing to follow wherever God leads you. May God's blessings shine through you every second of this day.

"But seek first his kingdom and his righteousness, and all these things will be given to you as well."
Matthew 6:33

TODAY'S PERSONAL MESSAGE
January 14th

*My prayer for you today is for you to open your heart
and mind and receive all the healing blessings that our
Heavenly Father has waiting for you.
May God bless and keep you all day and every day.*

*"I am with you and will watch over you wherever
you go, and I will bring you back to this land."*
Genesis 28:15

_____
_____
_____
_____
_____
_____

Today's Personal Message

January 15th

*My prayer for you today is to simply call out
"Help me Jesus!" and he will lift you up.
God bless and keep you all.*

*"No one has ever seen God; but if we love
one another, God lives in us and his
love is made complete in us."
John 4:12*

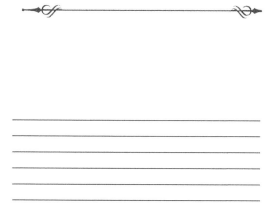

_____

_____

_____

_____

_____

_____

TODAY'S PERSONAL MESSAGE
January 16th

*My prayer for you today is that you know
in your heart and soul that God will never
leave you nor forsake you.
God bless you.*

*To this you were called, because Christ
suffered for you, leaving you an example
that you should follow in his steps.*
Peter 2:21

TODAY'S PERSONAL MESSAGE
January 17th

*My prayer for you today is to have a thankful heart and
enjoy God our Father's Presence in your life.
God bless us all.*

*You have made known to me the path of life;
you will fill me with joy in your presence,
with eternal pleasures at your right hand.
Palms 16:11*

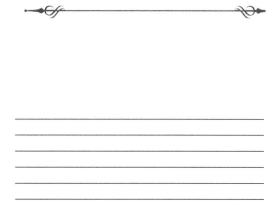

_____

_____

_____

_____

_____

_____

Today's Personal Message
January 18th

*My prayer for you today is to walk hand and
hand with the Father, stay on the path.
God bless you all.*

*And the peace of God, which transcends
all understanding, will guard your hearts
and your minds in Christ Jesus.
Philippians 4:7*

_____
_____
_____
_____
_____
_____

TODAY'S PERSONAL MESSAGE
January 19th

*My prayer for you today is to seek out God's special plan
for you. He has much in store for you.
May God bless your every move.*

*"So do not fear, for I am with you; do not
be dismayed, for I am your God. I will strengthen
you and help you; I will uphold you with my
righteous right hand."*
Isaiah 41:10

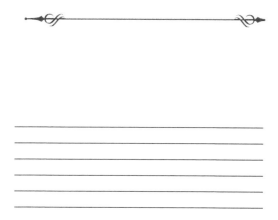

Today's Personal Message
January 20th

My Prayer for you today is to be filled with hope and always feel the touch of God's Healing Hand upon you. God bless and keep you.

"Those who know your name will trust in you, for you, Lord have never forsaken those who seek you."
Psalm 9:10

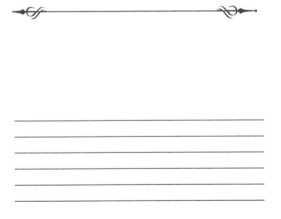

_____

_____

_____

_____

_____

_____

TODAY'S PERSONAL MESSAGE

January 21st

My prayer for you today is to not be afraid to let
God lead you. Stay on the Path.
God bless you and keep you.

"For I know the plans I have for you," declares the Lord,
"plans to prosper you and not harm you, plans to give you
hope and a future."
Jeremiah 29:11

TODAY'S PERSONAL MESSAGE
January 22nd

*My prayer for you today is for you to simply
Trust in God and receive His Love
and saving Power.*

*He who did not spare his own Son, but gave him up
for us all—how will he not also, along with him,
graciously give us all things?*
Romans 8:32

Today's Personal Message
January 23rd

My prayer for you today is to know that God our Father will never leave you, nor forsake you. God Bless you my friend.

"For I know the plans I have for you," declares the Lord, "Plans to prosper you and not harm you, plans to give you hope and a future."
Jeremiah 29:11

TODAY'S PERSONAL MESSAGE
January 24th

My prayer for you today is for you to believe in God's
healing mercy and receive His Endless Love.
May the Holy Spirit guide and bless you always.

"The heavens declare the glory of God; the skies
proclaim the work of his hands."
Psalm 19:1

_____
_____
_____
_____
_____
_____

Today's Personal Message
January 25th

My prayer for you today is to know God's
Love and Feel the Holy Spirit living in your soul.
God bless you.

Let the peace of Christ rule in your hearts, since as
members of one body you were called to peace.
And be thankful.
Colossians 3:15

_____

_____

_____

_____

_____

_____

TODAY'S PERSONAL MESSAGE
January 26th

My prayer for you today is to sit in silence and feel the power of God's Presence surrounding you! God bless you always and forever.

Whether you turn to the right or to the left, your ears will hear a voice behind you, saying, "This is the way; walk in it."
Isaiah 30:21

_____

_____

_____

_____

_____

_____

Today's Personal Message
January 27th

My prayer for you today is to trust in the Lord our God,
for He is the way and the light of your Life.
May God bless you all this day.

You have filled my heart with greater joy than when
their grain and new wine abound. I will lie down and
sleep in peace, for you alone, O Lord,
make me dwell in safety.
Psalm 4:7-8

_____
_____
_____
_____
_____
_____

TODAY'S PERSONAL MESSAGE
January 28th

*My prayer for you today is for you to know and
accept God's Presence in your heart. For His Love will
lead you places you never dreamed of.
God bless you.*

*"Keep your lives free from the love of money and be content
with what you have, because God has said, 'Never will I
leave you; never will I forsake you.'"*
Hebrews 13:5

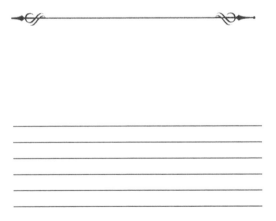

TODAY'S PERSONAL MESSAGE
January 29th

My prayer for you today is to know that you are anointed,
you are blessed, you are healthy, you are happy, you are
wealthy, and you are free of your addictions,
for all is possible through the Father,
the Son and the Holy Spirit.
God bless you.

Give all your worries and cares to God,
for he cares about you.
1 Peter 5:7

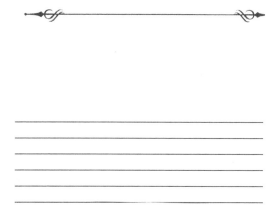

Today's Personal Message
January 30th

My prayer for you today is that you to feel
God's presence in all aspects of your life.
May God bless you and keep you safe.

He tends his flock like a shepherd: He gathers his lambs
in his arms and carries them close to his heart;
he gently leads those that have young.
Isaiah 40:11

_____
_____
_____
_____
_____
_____

Today's Personal Message

January 31st

*My prayer for you today is that you trust in God
our Father and believe in His word and let His
truth fill your life with Grace.
Blessings on you always!*

*"I am with you and will watch over you wherever you go,
and I will bring you back to this land."
Genesis 28:15*

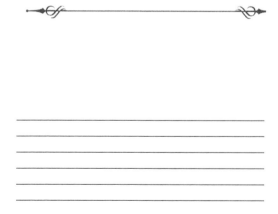

_____
_____
_____
_____
_____
_____

TODAY'S PERSONAL MESSAGE
February 1st

*My prayer for you today is to take life one step
at a time, trusting that the Holy Spirit is
walking beside you at all times.
Happy Birthday Kamala! I love you!
God Bless you.*

*Since we live by the Spirit, let us keep in
step with the spirit.
Galatians 5:25*

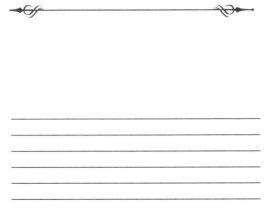

_____
_____
_____
_____
_____
_____

TODAY'S PERSONAL MESSAGE
February 2nd

*My prayer for you today is to know that healing
prayers are being sent to you today, close your
eyes and receive them.
God Bless you.*

*Dear friends, let us love one another, for love comes
from God. Everyone who loves has been born of God
and knows God. Whoever does not love does not know
God, because God is love.
John 4:7-8*

_____

_____

_____

_____

_____

_____

Today's Personal Message
February 3rd

My prayer for you today is to expect a healing in your life and graciously receive the blessings the Lord has set aside for you.
God bless you.

Now to him who is able to do immeasurably more than all we ask or imagine, according to his power that is at work within us.
Ephesians 3:20

_____

_____

_____

_____

_____

_____

TODAY'S PERSONAL MESSAGE
February 4th

My prayer for you today is that you continue to receive
and accept God's Love in your heart, for His Love is
unconditional and forever.
God Bless you.

For in Christ all the fullness of Deity lives in bodily form,
all you have been given fullness in Christ, who is the head
over every power and authority.
Colossians 2:9-10

_____

_____

_____

_____

_____

_____

Today's Personal Message
February 5th

My prayer for you today is to not be afraid,
to receive the Presence of the Holy Spirit in your life.
God is always with you.
God bless you.

But we all, with unveiled face, beholding as in a
mirror the glory of the Lord, are being transformed
into the same image from glory to glory, just as
by the Spirit of the Lord.
2 Corinthians 3:18

TODAY'S PERSONAL MESSAGE
February 6th

My prayer for you today is to know that God is in love with
you and has good things in store for you,
so believe in your miracle. Receive it.
God bless us all.

But I am like an olive tree flourishing in the house of God;
trust in God's unfailing love forever and ever.
Psalm 52:8

_____
_____
_____
_____
_____
_____

TODAY'S PERSONAL MESSAGE
February 7th

*My prayer for you today is that you receive the hope of
God's healing in your mind, body, and spirit and rejoice in
all of His Glorious Gifts. Amen
God bless you and May the Holy Spirit be with
you always.*

*For with you is the fountain of life;
in your light we see light.
Psalm 36:9*

Today's Personal Message
February 8th

*My prayer for you today is to learn to trust Jesus,
call out His Name! He will draw you near.
May God bless you.*

*Then Peter got down out of the boat, walked on the water
and came toward Jesus. But when he saw the wind, he was
afraid and, beginning to sink, cried out, "Lord, save me!"
Matthew 14:29-30*

_____
_____
_____
_____
_____
_____

TODAY'S PERSONAL MESSAGE
February 9th

My prayer for you today is for you to believe in the Lord our God. Be not afraid of anything for you belong to Him. God bless us all.

May the God of your hope so fill you with all joy and peace in believing [through the experience of your faith] that by the power of the Holy Spirit you may abound and be overflowing (bubbling over) with hope.
Romans 15:13

TODAY'S PERSONAL MESSAGE
February 10th

My prayer for you today is to walk in the
Light and Live God's plan for you.
May the Holy Spirit be with you always.

A light from on high will dawn upon [us] … to shine
upon and give light to those who sit in
darkness and in the shadow of death, to direct
and guide your feet…into the way of peace.
Luke 1:78-79

_____
_____
_____
_____
_____
_____

TODAY'S PERSONAL MESSAGE
February 11th

My prayer for you today is to never give up
the love you have in your heart for Jesus for
He will never give up on you.
May God bless you.

Before you know it, a sense of God's wholeness, everything
coming together for good, will come and settle you down.
It's wonderful what happens when Christ displaces at the
center of your life.
Philippians 4:7

TODAY'S PERSONAL MESSAGE
February 12th

My prayer for you today is to surrender your
heart and soul to our Savior Jesus Christ.
Expect Miracles in your life.
God bless each and every one of you.

"For God so loved the world that he gave his one and
only Son, that whoever believes in him shall not perish
but have eternal life."
John 3:16

_____
_____
_____
_____
_____
_____

TODAY'S PERSONAL MESSAGE
February 13th

*My prayer for you today is for you to not be afraid
of anything! For God's only begotten Son has paid
the price for your salvation.
God Bless you.*

*Even though I walk through the valley of the shadow
of death, I will fear no evil, for you are with me:
Your rod and your staff, they comfort me.
Psalm 23:4*

Today's Personal Message
February 14th

*My prayer for you today is that you do not give
into fear or worry. Lean on His Promises.
He is holding you by your right hand and
nothing can separate you from His love.
God Bless you.*

*Yet I am always with you; you hold me by my
right hand. You guide me with your counsel,
and afterward you will take me into glory.
Psalm 73:23-24*

Today's Personal Message
February 15th

*My prayer for you today is that you find the Healing and
Peace inside your heart and be thankful for all God's
blessings as you receive His Glorious Love.
God bless you and hold you.*

*"Blessed be he that cometh in the name of the Lord: we
have blessed you out of the house of the Lord."
Psalm 118:26*

Today's Personal Message
February 16th

My prayer for you today is to be still, be quiet,
and believe in His Healing Power.
May God bless you today and every day.

Rejoice evermore. Pray without ceasing.
In everything give thanks: for this is the will of
God in Christ Jesus concerning you.
1 Thessalonians 5:16-18

_____
_____
_____
_____
_____
_____

Today's Personal Message
February 17th

*My prayer for you today is to continue to
believe in God's most precious word and receive
His many gifts He has for you.
God bless you.*

*"So I say to you: ask and it will be given to you: seek and
you will find; knock and the door will be opened to you. for
everyone who ask receives; he who seeks finds;
and to him who knocks, the door will be opened."
Luke 11:9-10*

Today's Personal Message
February 18th

My prayer for you today is that you know in
your heart that God is always with you.
God bless you.

The Sovereign Lord has given me an instructed tongue,
to know the word that sustains the weary.
He awakens me morning by morning,
wakens my ear to listen like one being taught.
Isaiah 50:4

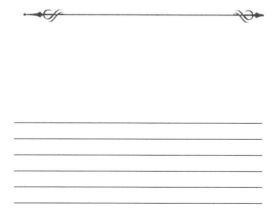

TODAY'S PERSONAL MESSAGE
February 19th

My prayer for you today is to never give up on the ones
you love, even when the gesture is not returned in kind.
God is watching and remembering.
God bless you always.

"For if you forgive people their trespasses,
your heavenly Father will also
forgive you."
Matthew 6:14

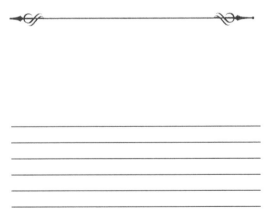

TODAY'S PERSONAL MESSAGE
February 20th

*My prayer for you today is that you believe in and
receive the miracle that God has in store for you.
God bless you.*

*"Whoever believes in me, as the scripture has said,
streams of living water will flow from within him."
John 7:38*

_____
_____
_____
_____
_____
_____

TODAY'S PERSONAL MESSAGE
February 21st

*My prayer for you today is to keep your eye on the Father
and the Son and the Holy Spirit, believing and trusting
in Him to protect you from all your worries. Amen!
God bless you and hold you.*

*Cast all your anxiety on Him because
He cares for you.
1 Peter 5:7*

TODAY'S PERSONAL MESSAGE
February 22nd

My prayer for you today is to ask God for your miracle,
constantly praising His Holy Name, giving Him thanks.
May the grace of God be with you always.

I can do all things through Him
who strengthens me.
Philippians 4:13

Today's Personal Message
February 23rd

My prayer for you today is for you to walk In His
Glorious Light, fixing your eyes on Jesus, trusting
that He knows your every next step.
God Bless you.

When I am afraid, I will trust in you. In God,
whose word I praise, in God I trust;
I will not be afraid.
What can mortal man do to me?
Psalm 56:3-4

_____
_____
_____
_____
_____
_____

Today's Personal Messag

February 24th

My prayer for you today is that you know that God's
strength will carry you through anything.
May His blessing be with you always.

"Remain in me, and I will remain in you.
No branch can bear fruit by itself;
it must remain in the vine. Neither can you
bear fruit unless you remain in me."
John 15:4

_____
_____
_____
_____
_____
_____

Today's Personal Message
February 25th

My prayer for you today is to have a grateful heart.
May God bless your every step.

For you know the grace of our Lord Jesus Christ, that
though he was rich, yet for your sakes he became poor,
so that through his poverty might become rich.
2 Corinthians 8:9

Today's Personal Message
February 26th

*My prayer for you today is that you believe with
all your heart and soul that God is leading you
right where you need to go.
May God bless you always.*

*In your unfailing love you will lead the people
you have redeemed. In your strength you will
guide them to your holy dwelling.
Exodus 15:13*

TODAY'S PERSONAL MESSAGE
February 27th

*My prayer for you today is to know that God is
always with you. May you receive His precious
blessings with an open heart.
God bless you!*

*May the God of hope fill you with all joy and peace as
you trust in him, so that you may overflow with hope
by the power of the Holy Spirit
Romans 15:13*

_____
_____
_____
_____
_____
_____

Today's Personal Message
February 28th

*My prayer for you today is to stop judging and
start believing in God's unconditional Love.
God bless you!*

*The Lord appeared to us in the past, saying
"I have loved you with an everlasting love;
I have drawn you with loving-kindness."
Jeremiah 31:3*

_____
_____
_____
_____
_____
_____

Today's Personal Message
February 29th

*My prayer for you today is to keep on the right path
and follow God's Loving lead, for He will be with you.
God bless and keep you.*

*"No one will be able to stand up against you all the days of
your life. As I was with Moses, so I will be with you; I will
never leave you nor forsake you… Have I not commanded
you? Be strong and courageous. Do not be terrified; do not
be discouraged, for the Lord your God will be with you
wherever you go."*
Joshua 1:5, 9

TODAY'S PERSONAL MESSAGE

March 1st

*My prayer for you today is to not take God's many gifts
for granted. He has blessed you with all you will ever
need. Give thanks for His Love.
God bless you.*

*Trust in the Lord with all your heart and
lean not on your own understanding;
in all your ways acknowledge him,
and he will make your path straight.
Proverbs 3:5-6*

_____
_____
_____
_____
_____
_____

Today's Personal Message
March 2nd

My prayer for you today is to trust in God's path
for you and follow wherever He leads you.
God bless you always.

"Come to me all you who are weary and burdened,
and I will give you rest. Take my yoke upon you
and learn from me, for I am gentle and humble in heart,
and you will find rest for your souls. For my yoke is easy
and my burden is light,"
Matthew 11:28-30

_____
_____
_____
_____
_____
_____

TODAY'S PERSONAL MESSAGE
March 3rd

*My prayer for you today is that you find your
way to the healing grace of our Lord.
God bless you.*

*Let us fix our eyes on Jesus, the author and
perfecter of our faith, who for the joy set before him
endured the cross, scorning its shame, and sat
down at the right hand of the throne of God.
Hebrews 12:2*

Today's Personal Message
March 4th

My prayer for you today is to not worry,
for God has a glorious plan for you.
God Bless you.

May the God of hope fill you with all joy and peace as you
trust in him, so that you may overflow with hope by the
power of the Holy Spirit.
Romans 15:13

Today's Personal Message
March 5th

My prayer for you today is that you know that
you belong to God in every way.
May God bless you always.

Always giving thanks to God the Father
for everything, in the name of our
Lord Jesus Christ.
Ephesians 5:20

TODAY'S PERSONAL MESSAGE
March 6th

*My prayer for you today is that you know that your
heart is always full when you have Jesus by your side.
Never doubt that He's always by your side.
God bless you always.*

*"Give thanks to the Lord, for he is good; his
love endures forever."*
Psalm 118:1

_____
_____
_____
_____
_____
_____

TODAY'S PERSONAL MESSAGE
March 7th

My prayer for you today is to stay
constantly in His healing Light.
God bless you all.

"Come to me, all you who are weary and burdened, and I
will give you rest. Take my yoke upon you and learn
from me, I am gentle and humble in heart, and you
will find rest for your souls."
Matthew 11:28-29

TODAY'S PERSONAL MESSAGE
March 8th

*My prayer for you today is to ask for God's
guidance and be truly thankful for His answer.
God bless you.*

*"So do not worry, saying, 'What shall we eat?' or, 'What
shall we drink?' or ' What shall we wear?' For the pagans
run after all these things, and your heavenly Father
knows that you need them."*
Matthew 6:31, 32

_____

_____

_____

_____

_____

_____

TODAY'S PERSONAL MESSAGE
March 9th

My prayer for you today is to live in God's light,
and His Light will shine brightly into the lives
of others through you.
God bless you and hold you.

Trust in the Lord and do good; dwell in the land
and enjoy safe pasture. Delight yourself in the Lord
and he will give you the desires of your heart.
Psalm 37:3-4

_____
_____
_____
_____
_____
_____

Today's Personal Message
March 10th

*My prayer for you today is to know that
the Father's way for you is perfect,
now and forever.
God bless you.*

*The word became flesh and made his dwelling among us.
We have seen his glory, the glory of the One and Only,
who came from the Father. Full of grace and truth.
John 1:14*

_____
_____
_____
_____
_____
_____

Today's Personal Message
March 11th

*My prayer for you today is to know that with God
by your side, you can accomplish anything.
God bless you.*

*"For this is good and acceptable in the sight of God
our Savior; who will have all men to be saved, and to
come unto the knowledge of the truth."*
Timothy 2:3-4

_____
_____
_____
_____
_____
_____

TODAY'S PERSONAL MESSAGE
March 12th

*My prayer for you today is to continue in
constant prayer and hope, for God's love and
salvation is filling your soul with life.
May God our Father bless you always.*

*This is the day that the Lord has made;
let us rejoice and be glad in it.
Psalm 118:24*

_____
_____
_____
_____
_____
_____

Today's Personal Message
March 13th

*My prayer for you today is to find the peace in your
troubled soul, for He has overcome the world for you.
God bless you.*

*For God, who said, "Let light shine out of darkness,"
made his light shine in our hearts to give us the light of
knowledge of the glory of God in the face of Christ.
2 Corinthians 4:6*

Today's Personal Message
March 14th

My prayer for you today is to know that there
is a healing coming, be still, believe
and receive God's glorious gifts
He has for you!
God bless you.

I am still confident of this: I will see the goodness
of the Lord in the land of the living. Wait for the Lord;
be strong and take heart and wait for the Lord.
Psalm 27:13-14

_____
_____
_____
_____
_____
_____

TODAY'S PERSONAL MESSAGE
March 15th

My prayer for you today is to not be afraid
to ask God for all you need.
He will hear you.
God bless you.

Now it is God who makes both us and you stand firm
in Christ. He anointed us, set his seal of ownership
on us, and put his Spirit in our hearts as a deposit,
guaranteeing what is to come.
2 Corinthians 1:21-22

TODAY'S PERSONAL MESSAGE
March 16th

My prayer for you today is to find God's
peace in your life and embrace it.
Bless you.

"Peace I leave with you; My Peace I give you.
I do not give to you as the world gives. Do not let
your hearts be troubled and do not be afraid."
John 14:27

_____
_____
_____
_____
_____
_____

Today's Personal Message
March 17th

My prayer for you today is to accept the forgiveness
God offers you in every breath you take.
God bless you.

Therefore, there is now no condemnation for those
who are in Christ Jesus, because through Christ Jesus
the law of the Spirit of life set me free from the
law of sin and death.
Romans 8:1-2

_____
_____
_____
_____
_____
_____

Today's Personal Message
March 18th

*My prayer for you today is to trust in
God's plan for you one day at a time.
May God bless you abundantly.*

*So we fix our eyes not on what is seen,
but on what is unseen. For what is seen is
temporary, but what is unseen is eternal.
2 Corinthians 4:18*

Today's Personal Message
March 19th

*My prayer for you today is to know with
all your heart and soul that you belong to Jesus.
God bless you.*

*To them God has chosen to make heaven known
among the Gentiles the glorious riches of this mystery,
which is Christ in you, the hope of glory.
Colossians 1:27*

_____
_____
_____
_____
_____
_____

Today's Personal Message
March 20th

My prayer for you today is to give up your fears and concentrate on the glorious blessings God has given you. God bless you.

Up to this time you have not asked a [single] thing in My Name [as presenting all I am]; but now ask and keep on asking and you will receive, so that your joy (gladness, delight) may be full and complete.
John 16:24

_____
_____
_____
_____
_____
_____

Today's Personal Message
March 21st

*My prayer for you today is to know that the Lord's
healing Power is unlimited in your life. Claim it!
God bless you.*

*Even in darkness light dawns for the upright,
for the gracious and compassionate and righteous
man.... He will have no fear of bad news;
his heart is steadfast, trusting in the Lord.
Psalm 112:4-7*

Today's Personal Message
March 22nd

*My prayer for you today is for you to know with all your
heart and soul that God loves you always.
God bless you now and forever!*

*The Lord your God is with you, he is mighty to save. He
will take great delight in you, he will quiet you with his
love, he will rejoice over you with singing.
Zephaniah 3:17*

_____
_____
_____
_____
_____
_____

Today's Personal Message
March 23rd

My prayer for you today is for you to give
your fears and anxieties to the Lord, for He
will take you by your right hand and make
you whole again.
God bless you.

Yes, I am always with you; you hold me by my
right hand. You guide me with your counsel,
and afterward you will take me into glory.
Psalm 73:23-24

TODAY'S PERSONAL MESSAGE
March 24th

*My prayer for you today is to know that our
Father will never leave you nor forsake you.
God bless you always.*

*"No one will be able to stand up against you all the
days of your life. As I was with Moses, so I will be
with you; I will never leave you nor forsake you."
Joshua 1:5*

Today's Personal Message
March 25th

My prayer for you today is to always
Remember to have a thankful heart.
God bless you.

So then, just as you received Christ Jesus as Lord,
continue to live in Him, strengthened in faith as
you were taught, and overflowing
with thankfulness.
Colossians 2:6-7

_____
_____
_____
_____
_____
_____

TODAY'S PERSONAL MESSAGE
March 26th

*My prayer for you today is to stay hopeful
in the word and in the promises of the Lord, for
He holds you in the palm of His hand.
God bless you now and forever.*

*For we are Gods workmanship, created in
Christ Jesus to do good works which God
prepared in advance for us to do.
Ephesians 2:10*

Today's Personal Message

March 27th

My prayer for you today is to know that Christ
has risen and is Alive in you!
Thank Him for His loving forgiveness!
God Bless you.

Trust in him at all times, O people;
pour out your hearts to him, for
God is our refuge.
Psalm 62:8

Today's Personal Message
March 28th

*My Prayer for you today is to know God and
keep Him close to you always and forever.
God bless you.*

*Come near to God and he will come near to you.
Wash your hands, you sinners, and purify your hearts,
you double-minded.*
James 4:8

_____

_____

_____

_____

_____

_____

TODAY'S PERSONAL MESSAGE
March 29th

*My prayer for you today is to slow down,
learn to take life one step at a time,
trusting in God's plan for you.
God bless you every step of the way.*

*We are assured and know that all things
work together and are [fitting into a plan] for
good to and for those who love God and are
called to [His] design and purpose.*
Romans 8:28

Today's Personal Message
March 30th

My prayer you today is that you learn
to trust God in every way.
God bless you always.

I say to myself, "The Lord is my portion;
therefore I will wait for him." The Lord is good
to those whose hope is in him, to the one who seeks
him; it is good to wait quietly for the
salvation of the Lord.
Lamentations 3:24-26

_____
_____
_____
_____
_____
_____

TODAY'S PERSONAL MESSAGE
March 31st

My prayer for you today is to remember to
thank God every day for
His Loving Peace.
God bless you and hold you.

But those who hope in the lord will renew their
strength. They will soar on wings like eagles; they
will run and not grow weary, they will walk
and not be faint.
Isaiah 40:31

Today's Personal Message
April 1st

My prayer for you today is to always stay
in the Light of His Love.
God bless you.

"I will never leave you nor forsake you…
Have I not commanded you? Be strong and courageous.
Do not be terrified; do not be discouraged, for the Lord
your God will be with you wherever you go."
Joshua 1:7,9

Today's Personal Message
April 2nd

*My prayer for you today is to trust God
to rid your heart of all your troubles.
God bless you.*

*Neither height nor depth, nor anything else in
all creation, will be able to separate us from the
love of God that is in Christ Jesus our Lord.
Romans 8:39*

_____
_____
_____
_____
_____
_____

TODAY'S PERSONAL MESSAGE
April 3rd

*My prayer for you today is for you to believe
that it is impossible for you to have any need
that Our Heavenly Father cannot meet.
God bless you always.*

*You will show me the path of life; in Your
Presence is fullness of joy; at Your right
hand are pleasures forevermore.
Psalm 16:11*

_____
_____
_____
_____
_____
_____

Today's Personal Message
April 4th

My prayer for you today is that your
heart is always filled with the joy
of God's Presence.
God bless you.

Let everything that has breath
praise the Lord. Praise the Lord
Psalm 150:6

Today's Personal Message
April 5th

My prayer for you today is to not be afraid,
for His forgiveness is your salvation.
Happy Birthday Amanda. I Love you!
God bless you.

But I trust in your unfailing love;
My heart rejoices in your salvation.
Psalm 13:5

Today's Personal Message
April 6th

*My prayer for you today is for you to always
walk in His Light and do not take for
granted life, salvation, sunshine, flowers,
and the countless gifts from God.
May God bless you forever.*

*As for God, his way is perfect; the word
of the Lord is flawless. He is a shield for all
who take refuge in Him.
Psalm 18:30*

TODAY'S PERSONAL MESSAGE
April 7th

My prayer for you today is to trust God
our Father to lead you in all the decisions
you make for your life. Amen
God bless you.

"So do not fear, for I am with you;
do not be dismayed, for I am your God.
I will strengthen you and help you;
I will uphold you with my righteous right hand."
Isaiah 41:10

Today's Personal Message
April 8th

My prayer for you today is that you never
forget that God's healing power is constantly
with you. Ask and you shall receive.
God Bless you.

The eternal God is your refuge, and underneath
are the everlasting arms. He will drive out
your enemy before you, saying, "Destroy him!"
Deuteronomy 33:27

Today's Personal Message
April 9th

*My prayer for you today is to choose to
practice God's Presence in your heart and
soul receiving God's healing power.
God bless you.*

*"I have told you these things, so that in
me you have peace. In this world you will
have trouble. But take heart!
I have overcome the world."*
John 16:33

_____
_____
_____
_____
_____
_____

Today's Personal Message
April 10th

*My prayer for you today is to know that you
do not have to be afraid of anything anymore,
for God is with you always.
God bless you now and forever.*

*The Lord God is with you, he is mighty to save.
He will take great delight in you, He will quiet you
with His love, He will rejoice over you with singing.
Zephaniah 3:17*

_____
_____
_____
_____
_____
_____

TODAY'S PERSONAL MESSAGE
April 11th

*My prayer for you today is to find the joy in
everything God has made for you, and do not
worry about tomorrow or yesterday.
God bless you.*

*God so loved the world that He gave His only
begotten Son, that whosoever believeth on his should not
perish but have everlasting life.
John 3:16*

_____

_____

_____

_____

_____

_____

TODAY'S PERSONAL MESSAGE
April 12th

My prayer for you today is a simple one.
Trust in the Lord and His ways, for
He will give you all you need.
God bless you always.

But if we walk in the light, as he is in the light,
we have fellowship with one another, and the
blood of Jesus, his Son purifies us from all sin.
John 1:7

_____
_____
_____
_____
_____
_____

TODAY'S PERSONAL MESSAGE
April 13th

*My prayer for you today is to walk
with God every step you take.
God bless you all.
Happy Birthday Mom. I Love You!*

*And my God will meet all your needs
according to his glorious riches
in Christ Jesus.
Philippians 4:19*

Today's Personal Message
April 14th

My prayer for you today is to live every
day in the Light of God's unfailing Love.
God bless you.

Be joyful always; pray continually; give
thanks in all circumstances, for this is
God's will for you in Christ Jesus.
1 Thessalonians 5:16-18

_____

_____

_____

_____

_____

_____

TODAY'S PERSONAL MESSAGE
April 15th

*My prayer for you today is to trust God's
plan for your life and don't be afraid.
God bless you.*

*"He is before all things, and in him all
things hold together."
Colossians 1:17*

Today's Personal Message
April 16th

My prayer for you today is to join me in
giving thanks for all of God's
wondrous deeds.
God bless you.

We are assured and know that [God being a partner in
their labor] all things work together and are
[fitting into a plan] for good to and for those
who love God and are called according to
[His] design and purpose.
Romans 8:28

_____
_____
_____
_____
_____
_____

TODAY'S PERSONAL MESSAGE
April 17th

*My prayer for you today is to stand in agreement
with God's loving course for you. Fear not,
for He is with you always.
God bless you.*

*"I am with you and will watch over you
wherever you go, and I will bring you back
to this land. I will not leave you until I have
done what I have promised you."*
Genesis 28:15

TODAY'S PERSONAL MESSAGE
April 18th

*My prayer for you today is to learn to live
each day with Christ Jesus and His promise
to never let us go.
God Bless you.*

*"Behold, the Lord God will come with strong hand,
and his arm shall rule for him: behold, his reward
is with him, and his work before him."*
Isaiah 40:10

Today's Personal Message
April 19th

My prayer for you today is to bring all your
anxieties to the Father and receive
His unfailing Love.
God bless you.

"Blessed are the poor in spirit, for theirs
is the kingdom of heaven. Blessed are those
who hunger and thirst for righteousness,
for they will be filled.
Matthew 5:3-6

_____
_____
_____
_____
_____
_____

Today's Personal Message
April 20th

*My prayer for you today is to know that you are never
alone, and that God will never leave you.
God bless you always.*

*Therefore, if anyone is in Christ, he is a new creation; the
old has gone, the new has come!
Corinthians 5:17*

Today's Personal Message
April 21st

My prayer for you today is to open yourself up to
God's loving Presence in every moment of your life
and receive His healing Spirit in your heart.
God Bless you.

"I am the vine; you are the branches. If a man
remains in me and I in him, he will bear much fruit;
apart from me you can do nothing."
John 15:5

_____
_____
_____
_____
_____
_____

Today's Personal Message
April 22nd

*My prayer for you today is that you close your eyes and
listen to God's voice quietly, thanking Him with every
beat of your heart for all that He does for you.
God bless and keep you.*

*Thou preparest a table before me in the
presence of mine enemies: thou anointest my
head with oil; my cup runneth over.
Psalm 23:5*

_____
_____
_____
_____
_____
_____

TODAY'S PERSONAL MESSAGE
April 23rd

*My prayer for you today is to keep your eyes
on the Lord, and know that he is always holding
you in his arms.
God bless you.*

*Those who look to him are radiant;
their faces are never covered with shame.
Psalm 34:5*

Today's Personal Message
April 24th

My prayer for you today is to rest in God's Presence knowing that He is always with you and you are in Him. God bless you always.

Do not conform any longer to the pattern of this world but be transformed by the renewing of your mind. Then you will be able to test and approve what God's will is- His good, and perfect will.
Romans 12:2

_____
_____
_____
_____
_____
_____

TODAY'S PERSONAL MESSAGE
April 25th

*My prayer for you today is to look to God our
Father and follow the steps He has laid before you.
God bless you.*

*"The one who sent me is with me: he has not left me alone,
for I always do what pleases him."
John 8:29*

TODAY'S PERSONAL MESSAGE
April 26th

*My prayer for you today is to give your problems and
sorrows over to your Loving God and receive the many
miracles and blessings He has waiting for you.
May God bless you always.*

*But we all, with unveiled face, beholding as in a mirror
the glory of the Lord, are being transformed into
the same image from glory to glory, just as by
the Spirit of the Lord.
2 Corinthians 3:18*

TODAY'S PERSONAL MESSAGE
April 27th

My prayer for you today is to not be afraid,
for God is with you every step of the way.
God bless you.

For He will give His angels [especial] over you to
accompany and defend and preserve you in all your ways
[of obedience and service]. They shall bear you up on their
hands, lest you dash your foot against a stone.
Psalm 91:11-12

Today's Personal Message
April 28th

*My prayer for you today is that God our Father will
grant all your needs, and for you to believe and receive
the miracles that He has in store for you.
God bless you.*

*Delight yourself in the Lord and he
will give you the desires of your heart.
Psalm 37:4*

_____
_____
_____
_____
_____
_____

TODAY'S PERSONAL MESSAGE
April 29th

My prayer for you today is to accept all
God's blessings with a thankful heart.
God bless you.

If the Lord delights in a man's ways,
he makes his steps firm; though he stumbles,
he will not fall, for the Lord upholds
him with his hand.
Psalm 37:23-24

_____
_____
_____
_____
_____
_____

TODAY'S PERSONAL MESSAGE
April 30th

*My prayer for you today is to live in the present moment
where God is always waiting to help you.
God bless and keep you.*

*Yet, O Lord, you are our Father. We are the clay, you are
the Potter; we are all the work of your hand.
Isaiah 64:8*

Today's Personal Message

May 1st

*My prayer for you today is to always remember
that God walks with you every step of your life,
holding you By His Right Hand.
May God bless you.*

*Now to him who is able to do immeasurably more
than all we ask or imagine, according to his power
that is at work within us.*
Ephesians 3:20

Today's Personal Message
May 2nd

*My prayer for you today is that you
learn the ways of the Lord. Depend on
Him for He will give you Life.
May God bless you all.*

*He who did not spare his own Son, but gave
him up for us all—how will he not also,
along with him, graciously give us all things?
Romans 8:32*

_____
_____
_____
_____
_____
_____

Today's Personal Message
May 3rd

*My prayer for you today is to remember
that Christ has your best interest at heart,
and He will always keep you safe.
Pray to Him.
May God bless you always.*

*"The one who sent me is with me;
he has not left me alone, for I always
do what pleases him."
John 8:29*

_____
_____
_____
_____
_____
_____

Today's Personal Message

May 4th

My prayer for you today is to believe in Christ Jesus for
He is with you always, holding you in His loving arms.
Receive your miracle!
May God bless you.

Praise the Lord, Praise the Lord, O my soul.
I will praise the Lord all my life;
I will sing praise to my God as long as I live.
Psalm 146:1-2

TODAY'S PERSONAL MESSAGE
May 5th

My prayer for you today is to receive
His Healing Power and give thanks
with every Breath you take.
May God bless you.

He makes me lie down in green pastures;
He leads me beside the still waters.
He restores my soul; He leads me in the paths of
righteousness for His name's sake.
Psalm 23:2-3

_____
_____
_____
_____
_____
_____

Today's Personal Message
May 6th

*My prayer for you today is for you to relax and focus
your attention on God's Presence in your life.
May God bless you.*

*My heart says of you, "Seek his face!"
your face Lord, I will seek.
Psalm 27:8*

Today's Personal Message
May 7th

*My prayer for you today is to trust God and do not fear anything, for He can deliver you from all harm.
May God bless you.*

*The righteous cry out and the Lord hears them; he delivers them from all their troubles.
Psalm 34:17*

_____
_____
_____
_____
_____
_____

Today's Personal Message
May 8th

*My prayer for you today is to remember that your
problems and your pain become small when Jesus is
holding your hand. Believe in Him, for
He will never let you go.
May God bless you always.*

*Now to him who is able to do immeasurably
more than all we ask or imagine, according
to his power that is at work within us.
Ephesians 3:20*

_____

_____

_____

_____

_____

_____

Today's Personal Message
May 9th

*My prayer for you today is to no longer dwell on
the past or the future. Stay in the moment with the
Father, the Son and the Holy Spirit.
May God bless you.*

*"These things I have spoken to you, that in
Me you may have peace. In the world you
will have tribulation; but be of good cheer,
I have overcome the world."
John 16:33*

_____
_____
_____
_____
_____
_____

TODAY'S PERSONAL MESSAGE
May 10th

*My prayer for you today is to see the difficulties
in your life as blessings that bring you closer
to God's healing power.
May God bless you.*

*"I am with you and will watch over you
wherever you go, and I will bring you back to
this land. I will not leave you until I have done
what I Have promised you."
Genesis 28:15*

TODAY'S PERSONAL MESSAGE
May 11th

*My prayer for you today is to not be
afraid to bring you problems to the Lord,
for in Him all things are healed.
God bless you.*

*For our light and momentary troubles
are achieving for us an eternal glory
that far outweighs them all.
2 Corinthians 4:17*

_____

TODAY'S PERSONAL MESSAGE
May 12th

My prayer for you today is to take time to rest in God's
merciful Love and let Him restore your heart.
God bless you now and forever.

"The Lord is gracious and compassionate
slow to anger and rich in love."
Psalms 145:8

Today's Personal Message
May 13th

*My prayer for you today is to let God
lead you in every step you take,
trusting Him, always being thankful
for His many gifts.
God bless you.*

*Whatever you do, work at it with all your
heart, as working for the Lord, not for men.
Colossians 3:23*

Today's Personal Message
May 14th

*My prayer for you today is to know in
your heart and your soul that there is
nothing too difficult for God to heal.
God bless you.*

*God is our Refuge and Strength
[mighty and impenetrable to temptation],
a very present and well-proved help in trouble.
Psalm 46:1*

Today's Personal Message
May 15th

*My prayer for you today is to take
time to be with God and He will be with
you. He will always shield you
from all your troubles.
God bless you.*

*The eternal God is your refuge, and underneath
are the everlasting arms. He will drive out your
enemy before you, saying "Destroy him!"*
Deuteronomy 33:27

_____
_____
_____
_____
_____
_____

Today's Personal Message

May 16th

*My prayer for you today is to realize that God
has been with you every step of the way, and
He is with you now, forever and always.
God bless you.*

*What, then, shall we say in response to this?
If God is for us, who can be against us?
Romans 8:31*

_____
_____
_____
_____
_____
_____

TODAY'S PERSONAL MESSAGE
May 17th

*My prayer for you today is to remember
that God's blessings are endless. Live by faith
and know He is always with you.
God bless you.*

*We live by faith, not by sight.
2 Corinthians 5:7*

Today's Personal Message

May 18th

My prayer for you today is to surrender
to the ways planned out by God our Father
and receive His many blessings.
God bless you all.

But we have this treasure in earthen vessels,
so that the surpassing greatness of the power
will be of God and not from ourselves.
2 Corinthians 4:7

_____
_____
_____
_____
_____
_____

Today's Personal Message
May 19th

*My prayer for you today is to have
faith in God's promises. When you lose sight
of His Love, seek Him and you will find all
the Blessings He has for you.
God bless you.*

*Give thanks in all circumstances, for this
is God's will for you in Christ and Jesus.
Thessalonians 5:18*

_____
_____
_____
_____
_____
_____

TODAY'S PERSONAL MESSAGE

May 20th

My prayer for you today is to stay in
His Light. Come out of the darkness and
find the path to a healing life.
God bless you.

For our light and momentary troubles
are achieving for us an eternal glory that
far outweighs them all.
2 Corinthians 4:17

Today's Personal Message

May 21st

*My prayer for you today is to be patient
in hope for the Lord God will take care of
your every need.
God bless you.*

*For with you is the fountain of life;
in your light we see light.
Psalm 36:9*

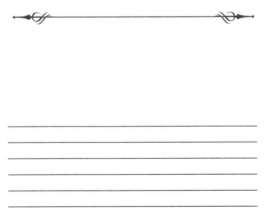

Today's Personal Message

May 22nd

*My prayer for you today is to remember
that even though things might be beyond your
understanding, God always has a perfect
plan for everything in your life.
God bless you.*

*Consider it pure joy, my brothers,
whenever you face trials of many kinds.
James 1:2*

_____
_____
_____
_____
_____
_____

TODAY'S PERSONAL MESSAGE

May 23rd

*My prayer for you today is to search and
find the hidden treasures God has placed
before you today and know that He is
holding you by the hand every step of the way.
God bless you.*

*"This is the day which the Lord hath made;
we will rejoice and be glad in it."*
Psalm 118:24

Today's Personal Message
May 24th

My prayer for you today is to be still
and listen. Let the Lord our God speak to you
and show you the way to eternal happiness.
Trust that He will never let you go.
God bless you.

"Be still before the Lord, all mankind,
because he has roused himself
from his holy dwelling."
Zechariah 2:13

_____
_____
_____
_____
_____
_____

TODAY'S PERSONAL MESSAGE
May 25th

*My prayer for you today is to ask God
for His healing Presence to come upon you.
Remember that He will uphold you
always. Ask and it shall be given to you.
God bless you now and forever.*

*Immediately, something like scales fell
from Saul's eyes, and he could see again.
He got up and was baptized.*
Acts 9:18

TODAY'S PERSONAL MESSAGE
May 26th

My prayer for you today is to know
this one undisputed truth. With
God nothing is impossible.
God bless you always.

"For in him we live and move and have our
being." As some of your own poets have said,
"We are his offspring."
Acts 17:28

TODAY'S PERSONAL MESSAGE
May 27th

*My prayer for you today is to ask the Holy Spirit to
control your thinking and be guided into the
Father's healing Light.
God bless you.*

*Blessed are those who have learned to acclaim you, who
walk in the light of your presence, Oh Lord.
Psalm 89:15*

Today's Personal Message
May 28th

*My prayer for you today is for you to declare
all of God's glorious gifts in your life and receive His
Healing Power upon your spirit. Amen.
God bless you.*

*The Sovereign Lord is my strength;
he makes my feet like the feet of the deer.
He enables me to go on the heights.
Habakkuk 3:19*

Today's Personal Message

May 29th

My prayer for you today is to be your best!
For God is always His best for you.
God bless you always.

Even there your hand will guide me;
your right hand will hold me fast.
Psalm 139:10

TODAY'S PERSONAL MESSAGE
May 30th

*My prayer for you today is for you to
spend all of today's precious moments
with God your Father and receive all the
Peace and Love He has in store for you.
God bless you.*

*Give unto the Lord the glory due His name;
worship the Lord in the beauty of holiness.*
Psalm 29:2

TODAY'S PERSONAL MESSAGE

May 31st

*My prayer for you today is to learn
to relax, close your eyes and be still in God's
Peace, and receive His healing blessings.
God bless you.*

*The Lord replied, "My Presence will go
with you, and I will give you rest."
Exodus 33:14*

TODAY'S PERSONAL MESSAGE

June 1st

My prayer for you today is to not fear
anything. Keep God in your heart, mind,
and soul every minute of this day.
He will guide your steps and always keep you safe.
God bless you.

Fear of man will prove to be a snare,
but whoever trust in the Lord is kept safe.
Proverbs 29:25

_____
_____
_____
_____
_____
_____

Today's Personal Message
June 2nd

*My prayer for you today is to learn to
be quiet, let go, relax, and be still so you
will know when He comes into your heart
and heals your troubled soul.
God bless you now and forever.*

*Humble yourselves, therefore, under God's
mighty hand, that he may lift you up in due time.
Cast your anxiety on him because he cares for you.
1 Peter 5:6-7*

_____
_____
_____
_____
_____
_____

Today's Personal Message
June 3rd

*My prayer for you today is simple. Ask for God's
Healing Presence to come into your life and
receive it with an open heart.
God bless you all.*

*Do not be anxious about anything,
but in everything, by prayer and
petition, with thanksgiving, present
your request to God.
Philippians 4:6*

_____
_____
_____
_____
_____
_____

TODAY'S PERSONAL MESSAGE

June 4th

*My prayer for you today is to always
remember that anything is possible
when you hold on to God's saving Grace.
God bless you.*

*You have made known to me the path
of life; you will fill me with joy in your
presence, with eternal pleasures at
your right hand.*
Psalm 16:11

_____
_____
_____
_____
_____
_____

TODAY'S PERSONAL MESSAGE
June 5th

*My prayer for you today is to love God
with all your heart and soul and seek His help and
guidance and it will be given to you.
God bless you all.*

*And that you may love the Lord your God,
listen to his voice, and hold fast to him.
For the Lord is your life, and he will give
you many years in the land he swore to give
to your fathers, Abraham, Isaac and Jacob.
Deuteronomy 30:20*

Today's Personal Message
June 6th

My prayer for you today is show kindness to others in everything you do, be that beacon of light that heals each other, and in return heals you.
God bless you.

But if we walk in the light, as he is in the light, we have fellowship with one another, and the blood of Jesus, his Son, purifies us from all sin.
John 1:7

TODAY'S PERSONAL MESSAGE
June 7th

My prayer for you today is to believe in the power of
prayer. Ask and you will receive. For God is
always with you.
May God bless you.

"I am the vine; you are the branches. If a man remains in
Me and I in him, he will bear much fruit; apart from
Me you can do nothing."
John 15:5

TODAY'S PERSONAL MESSAGE
June 8th

*My prayer for you today is to know that
you belong to Jesus and nothing can harm
you. Call out His name and receive God's
healing through the Blessed Holy Spirit.
God bless you.*

*"For nothing is impossible with God."
Luke 1:37*

Today's Personal Message
June 9th

My prayer for you today is to place a prayer cover over yourselves and over your children and ask God for His mighty healing power to come upon you.
May God bless you all.

Peace be with you; My peace I give you. I do not give to you as the world gives. Do not let your hearts be troubled and do not be afraid."
John 14:27

Today's Personal Message
June 10th

*My prayer for you today is to stay in the
moment, constant in prayer, knowing you are
in God's mighty hands.
God bless you.*

*I pray that out of his glorious riches he may
strengthen you with power through his Spirit
in your inner being, so that Christ may
dwell in your hearts through faith. And I pray
that you, being rooted and established in love…*
Ephesians 3:16-17

Today's Personal Message
June 11th

My prayer for you today is to always trust God's plan for you, stay constant in His Light. You don't have to be afraid, for He is your strength.
God bless you.

"Come to me, all you who are burdened, and I will give you rest. Take my yoke upon you and learn from me, for I am gentle and humble in heart, and you will find rest for your souls."
Matthew 11:28-29

TODAY'S PERSONAL MESSAGE
June 12th

*My prayer for you today is to stay alert to God's Presence
in your life and be thankful for His many blessings.
God bless you always.*

*Therefore by Him let us continually offer the sacrifice of
praise to God, that is, the fruit of our lips, giving
thanks to His name.*
Hebrews 13:15

Today's Personal Message
June 13th

My prayer for you today is for you to let God's healing power work through you. Ask Him to heal the others around you and in return He will heal you too. God bless you all.

This is the message we have heard from him and declare to you: God is light; in him there is no darkness at all.
1 John 1:5

_____
_____
_____
_____
_____
_____

TODAY'S PERSONAL MESSAGE
June 14th

*My prayer for you today is for you to feel God
lifting you up, out of despair, into His Loving Light!
Right where you need to be.
God bless you.*

*"Peace be with you; My peace I give you. I do not
give to you as the world gives. Do not let your hearts
be troubled and do not be afraid."
John 14:27*

Today's Personal Message
June 15th

*My prayer for you today is for you to close your eyes and spend a few quiet moments with God in deep awareness of His Power, Forgiveness, and Love.
God bless you.*

Though you have not seen him, you love him; and even though you do not see him now, you believe in him and are filled with an inexpressible and glorious joy.
1 Peter 1:8

_____
_____
_____
_____
_____
_____

Today's Personal Message

June 16th

My prayer for you today is to know that God has a plan for you. It is the right plan. Stay on the path and trust that He is always with you.
God bless you.

"So do not fear, for I am with you; do not be dismayed, for I am your God. I will strengthen you and help you; I will uphold you with my righteous right hand."
Isaiah 41:10

TODAY'S PERSONAL MESSAGE
June 17th

*My prayer for you today is to let God take the weight of
the world off your shoulders and for God's sake Laugh!
God Bless you always*

*And my God will meet your needs according to his
glorious riches in Christ Jesus.
Philippians 4:19*

_____

_____

_____

_____

_____

_____

Today's Personal Message

June 18th

My prayer for you today is to trust that
God has a perfect plan for you.
God bless you.

What then, shall we say in response to this?
If God is for us, who can be against us?
He who did not spare his own Son, but gave
him up for us all—how will he not also,
along with him, graciously give us all things?
Romans 8:31-32

_____

_____

_____

_____

_____

_____

TODAY'S PERSONAL MESSAGE
June 19th

*My prayer for you today is to always keep your eyes on
Jesus and hold tightly to His Hand for He will never leave
you nor forsake you.
God bless you and keep you.*

*Give unto the Lord the glory due to His name;
worship the Lord in the beauty of holiness.
Psalm 29:2*

TODAY'S PERSONAL MESSAGE
June 20th

My prayer for you today is to always love yourself
and each other as Jesus loves you and remember
that he will always be by your side.
God bless you and keep you.

I will offer You the sacrifice of thanksgiving
and will call on the name of the Lord.
Psalm 116:17

_____
_____
_____
_____
_____
_____

Today's Personal Message

June 21st

*My prayer for you today is to not worry about
anything, God is holding you by your right hand,
and He will never let you go.
God bless you.*

*Now to him who is able to do immeasurably more than all
we ask or imagine, according to his power that is at work
within us, to him be glory in the church and in Christ
Jesus throughout all generations, forever! Amen
Ephesians 3: 20-21*

Today's Personal Message
June 22nd

*My prayer for you today is to be in constant thanksgiving
to God for all things, for He is there for you all the time.
God bless you.*

*Let the peace of Christ rule in your hearts, since as
members of one body you were called to peace.
And be thankful.
Colossians 3:15*

TODAY'S PERSONAL MESSAGE

June 23rd

My prayer for you today is to know that with
God by your side you never have to be alone.
This is His promise to you always.
God bless you and keep you.

Even though I walk through
the valley of the shadow of death,
I will fear no evil, for you are with me;
your rod and your staff, they comfort me.
Psalm 23:4

Today's Personal Message

June 24th

My prayer for you today is to not be shaken by any
problems or dilemmas that come your way, for
God is always with you, and He will never let you go.
God bless you.

The Lord gives strength to his people; the
Lord blesses his people with peace.
Psalm 29:11

_____
_____
_____
_____
_____
_____

TODAY'S PERSONAL MESSAGE

June 25th

*My prayer for you today is to receive
the Healing Presence of God in your heart
and soul for He is always with you. Sing a new
song and rejoice giving thanks.
God bless you every day.*

*Let us come before him with thanksgiving
and extol him with music and song.
Psalm 95:2*

_____

_____

_____

_____

_____

_____

Today's Personal Message

June 26th

*My prayer for you today is for you to
close your eyes and feel God's Presence all
around you and give thanks to Him as his
healing power washes over you.
God bless you.*

*The Lord replied, "My Presence
will go with you, and I will give you rest."*
Exodus 33:14

Today's Personal Message

June 27th

*My prayer for you today is to always believe in God, even
when hard times seem to make you doubt your faith.
Hang on to His Love deep inside you, for He will
always be with you, and He will always Love you.
God bless you.*

*But as far as me, I watch in hope
for the Lord, I wait for God my
Savior; my God will hear me.
Micah 7:7*

TODAY'S PERSONAL MESSAGE
June 28th

My prayer for you today is to constantly walk in faith and hope knowing that your prayers will be answered. God bless you.

The Lord your God is with you, he is mighty to save. He will take great delight in you, he will quiet you with his love, he will rejoice over you with singing.
Zephaniah 3:17

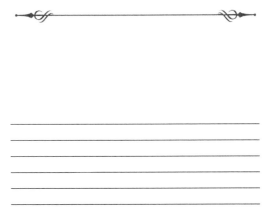

_____
_____
_____
_____
_____
_____

TODAY'S PERSONAL MESSAGE
June 29th

My prayer for you today is to be healed
of all of your afflictions, in the name of the
Father, the Son and the Holy Spirit. Remember
that with Him all things are possible.
God bless you.

Blessed are those who have learned to
acclaim you, who walk in the light
of your presence. O Lord.
Psalm 89:15

Today's Personal Message

June 30th

*My prayer for you today is to not be
afraid to let the Holy Spirit work in
your life. Do not be afraid to ask for help.
And do not be afraid to receive all the
blessings He is giving you.
God bless you.*

*Now may the Lord of peace himself give
you peace at all times and in every way.
The Lord be with all of you.*
2 Thessalonians 3:16

_____
_____
_____
_____
_____
_____

Today's Personal Message
July 1st

*My prayer for you today is find that special place in
your heart and soul where God is always present.
Spend time with Him and receive all the many gifts
He has for you.
God bless you.*

*"The Lord bless you and keep you; the Lord make his face
shine upon you and be gracious to you; the Lord turn his
face toward you and give you peace."
Numbers 6:24-26*

Today's Personal Message
July 2nd

*My prayer for you today is to learn to pray about all
things in your heart that you want and need and
know that God is always listening. Be patient,
for the right answers will come.
God bless you always.*

*To them God has chosen to make
known among the Gentiles the glorious
riches of this mystery, which is Christ
in you, the hope of glory.
Colossians 1:27*

_____
_____
_____
_____
_____
_____

TODAY'S PERSONAL MESSAGE
July 3rd

*My prayer for you today is to stop judging yourselves
and one another so harshly. The forgiveness you feel
in your heart is God forgiving you of your sins.
Receive it with open arms.
God bless you.*

*In addition to all this, take up the shield of faith,
with which you can extinguish all the flaming
arrows of the evil one.*
Ephesians 6:16

TODAY'S PERSONAL MESSAGE
July 4th

*My prayer for you today is for you to stay in close
contact with the Father, thanking Him for all His
blessings, past, present and future.
God bless you always.*

*Do not conform any longer to the pattern of this world
but be transformed by the renewing of your mind. Then
you will be able to test and approve what God's
will is—his good, pleasing and perfect will.*
Romans 12:2

Today's Personal Message
July 5th

*My prayer for you today is to let go of all those fears
that have you scared to death, stop clinging to the way
you think it should be. Trust in the power of God and
claim His healing power that belongs to you.
God bless you*

*But as for me, I watch in hope for the Lord, I wait for God
my Savior; my God will hear me.
Micah 7:7*

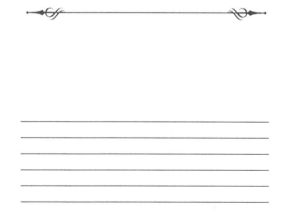

Today's Personal Message
July 6th

My prayer for you today is to know that with God in your heart you are always standing on Holy Ground. God bless you now and forever.

"No one will be able to stand up against you all the days of your life. As I was with Moses, So I will be with you; I will never leave you nor forsake you."
Joshua 1:5

TODAY'S PERSONAL MESSAGE

July 7th

*My prayer for you today is to practice trusting God and
thanking Him for all the special gifts He has for you.
Now receive them.
God bless you.*

*Rejoice in the Lord always. I will say it again: Rejoice!
Let your gentleness be evident to all. The Lord is near.
Do not be anxious about anything, but in everything,
by prayer and petition, with thanksgiving,
present your request to God.
Philippians 4:4-6*

Today's Personal Message
July 8th

My prayer for you today is to close your eyes and
Ask God for His forgiveness and His blessing with all your
heart and soul. Believe and Receive for He
will never let you down.
God bless you.

Surely God is my salvation; I will trust and not be afraid.
The Lord, the Lord himself, is my strength and my song; he has
become my salvation.
Isaiah 12:2

_____
_____
_____
_____
_____
_____

Today's Personal Message
July 9th

*My prayer for you today is to let yourself be
reprogrammed by God. Listen and hear His voice
advising and healing your mind.
God bless you all.*

*For we are God's workmanship, created in
Christ Jesus to do good works, which God
prepared in advance for us to do.
Ephesians 2:10*

_____
_____
_____
_____
_____
_____

Today's Personal Message
July 10th

My prayer for you today is this. Love yourself, love your friends, and above all love your God who holds you in the palm of his hands. Blessed be the one that loves all. God bless you all.

"I have told you these things, so that in me you may have peace. In this world you will have trouble. But take heart! I have overcome the world."
John 16:33

_____
_____
_____
_____
_____
_____

TODAY'S PERSONAL MESSAGE
July 11th

My prayer for you today is to remember to seek the
Father always and not only the things of this world.
For He is the Salvation, the Light and the Way!
God bless you.

The Lord appeared to us in the past, saying:
"I have loved you with an everlasting love;
I have drawn you with loving-kindness."
Jeremiah 31:3

TODAY'S PERSONAL MESSAGE
July 12th

My prayer for you today is to be a soldier for Christ. Take up His sword and proclaim His mighty Name! Thank Him for all things, for His blessings and healings await you.
Just ask and receive.
God bless you all.

I can do everything through him who gives me strength.
Philippians 4:13

TODAY'S PERSONAL MESSAGE
July 13th

*My prayer for you today is for you to take time
and listen closely to God's message for you,
remembering that He loves you no matter what,
and thankfully receive His healing power.
God bless you.*

*The heavens declare the glory of God; the skies proclaim
the work of his hands. Day after day they pour forth
speech; night after night they display knowledge.
Psalm 19:1-2*

TODAY'S PERSONAL MESSAGE
July 14th

My prayer for you today is for you to stay
constant in prayer, making your journey in
this life a safe path to heaven.
May God bless us all.

But let all who take refuge in you be glad; let them
ever sing for joy. Spread your protection over them
that those who love your name may rejoice in you.
Psalm 5:11

_____
_____
_____
_____
_____
_____

Today's Personal Message
July 15th

My prayer for you today is to not worry about
anything, for God will always have your back.
Trust in Him at all times.
God bless you.

There is no fear in love. But perfect
love drives out fear, because fear has to do
with punishment. The one who fears
is not made perfect in Love.
1 John 4:18

TODAY'S PERSONAL MESSAGE
July 16th

*My prayer for you today is for you to listen
to God's message even when it is hard to hear.
Trust in Him always for He listens to your every
prayer and knows your every need.
God bless you.*

*Be strong and courageous. Do not be afraid
or terrified because of them, for the Lord your
God goes with you; he will never leave you
nor forsake you.
Deuteronomy 31:6*

Today's Personal Message
July 17th

My prayer for you today is to always remember
to spend time with God our Father every
chance you get, for one day it will be
too late to get the chance.
God bless you.

O God, you are my God; early I will seek you;
my soul thirst for you; my flesh longs for you
in a dry thirsty land where there is no water.
Psalm 63:1

TODAY'S PERSONAL MESSAGE
July 18th

*My prayer for you today is for you to know
in your heart and soul that God is always closer
to you than you think. Receive His Loving,
healing Presence that is always waiting for you.
May God bless you in ways you never dreamed of.*

*"I am with you and will watch over you wherever you go,
and I will bring you back to this land. I will not leave you
until I have done what I have promised you."*
Genesis 28:15

TODAY'S PERSONAL MESSAGE
July 19th

*My prayer for you today is this; when you
feel fear and anxieties consuming you, Stop!
And whisper His Precious Name saying
Jesus help me. And He will hold you in
His loving arms and give you Peace.
Amen God bless you.*

*Now may the Lord of peace himself give
you peace at all times and every way.
The Lord be with all of you.
2 Thessalonians 3:16*

Today's Personal Message
July 20th

*My prayer for you today is to shine brightly,
so others can see your faith, and learn from
the Light of God that radiates from you.
God bless you always.*

*Therefore we do not lose heart. Though
outwardly we are wasting away, yet inwardly
we are being renewed day by day. For our
light and momentary troubles are achieving for
us an eternal glory that far outweighs them all.*
2 Corinthians 4:16-17

_____
_____
_____
_____
_____
_____

TODAY'S PERSONAL MESSAGE
July 21st

My prayer for you today is that even when
you don't understand God's message and you
are confused about life, that's when you need to trust in
God's plan for you even more. Lean on Him,
trust and be confident. He will be your strength.
God Bless you.

Consider it pure joy, my brothers,
whenever you face trials of many kinds.
James 1:2

TODAY'S PERSONAL MESSAGE
July 22nd

My prayer for you today is to stay close to God always knowing that He is everything, and God bless you with every Breath you take.

I delight greatly in the Lord; my soul rejoices in my God. For he has clothed me with garments of salvation and arrayed me in a robe of righteousness, as a bridegroom adorns his head like a priest, and as a bride adorns herself with her jewels.
Isaiah 61:10

_____
_____
_____
_____
_____
_____

TODAY'S PERSONAL MESSAGE
July 23rd

My prayer for you today is to always have the
"I am" in your life. When you ask for God's
Great gifts, always begin your prayers with I am.
"I am anointed, I am blessed, I am healthy, I am
happy, I am healed." Remember you are always the
"I am" in His beautiful Light.
God bless you.

"I am the Alpha and the Omega," says the Lord God,
who is, and who was, and who is to come, the Almighty."
Revelations 1:8

_____
_____
_____
_____
_____
_____

TODAY'S PERSONAL MESSAGE
July 24th

*My prayer for you today is to rejoice in
God's many blessings and be thankful especially
for his gifts of love and healing.
God bless you.*

*As for God, His way is perfect; the word
of the Lord is flawless. He is a shield for
all who take refuge in him.
Psalm 18:30*

TODAY'S PERSONAL MESSAGE
July 25th

My prayer for you today is to listen to God.
Really listen to Him because he is always reaching
out to you. Seek Him constantly. Listen and receive
His marvelous Blessings.
May God bless you today and every day.

You will keep in perfect peace with him whose mind is
steadfast, because he trusts in you.
Isaiah 26:3

TODAY'S PERSONAL MESSAGE
July 26th

My prayer for you today is for you to learn
to trust in God's word, stay in constant prayer
and hope, and never ever stop loving Him first and always.
He always has the answers you need.
He will heal your broken life.
God bless you.

"The wind blows wherever it pleases. You hear
it's sound, but you cannot tell where it comes
from or where it is going. So it is with
everyone born of the Spirit."
John 3:8

Today's Personal Message

July 27th

*My prayer for you today is to remember
to Never Give up Hope, for God will never leave
your side or ever let go of your right hand.
You are a child of God. You belong to Him.
God bless you.*

*"So do not fear, for I am with you; do not be
dismayed, for I am your God. I will strengthen
you and help you; I will uphold you with
My righteous right hand."*
Isaiah 41:10

Today's Personal Message
July 28th

*My prayer for you today is to always remember that
Jesus has you by the right hand and will never let go.
God bless you all.*

*The Lord is my shepherd, I shall not be in want. He makes
me lie down in green pastures, he leads me beside quiet
waters, He restores my soul. He guides me in paths of
righteousness for His name's sake. Even though I walk
through the valley of death, I will fear no evil, for you are
with me; your rod and your staff, they comfort me.
Psalm 23:1-4*

_____

_____

_____

_____

_____

_____

Today's Personal Message
July 29th

*My prayer for you today is to keep your heart
and soul on a short rope as to not get too far from God's
Healing Presence and if you do, just give a little tug.
God bless you.*

*Delight yourself in the Lord and he will
give you the desires of your heart.
Psalm 37:4*

_____
_____
_____
_____
_____
_____

TODAY'S PERSONAL MESSAGE
July 30th

*My prayer for you today is to open your eyes
and see all the beauty around you and the
wonder of God's many blessings He has for you.
Open your mind and heart and receive
these wonderful gifts.
God bless you.*

*In everything give thanks; for this
is God's will for you in Christ Jesus.
1 Thessalonians 5:18*

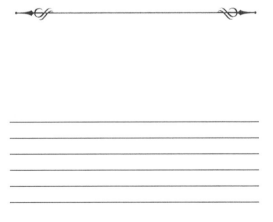

Today's Personal Message

July 31st

My prayer for you today is to stop being afraid
and worrying all the time. Break the grip of fear by
reminding yourself that God is with you always.
Forgive yourself as He has forgiven you.
God bless you

There is no fear in love. But perfect
love drives out fear, because fear has
to do with punishment. The one who fears
is not made perfect in love.
1 John 4:18

_____
_____
_____
_____
_____
_____

TODAY'S PERSONAL MESSAGE

August 1st

My prayer for you today is to pray to the Lord our God for a healing in your heart, mind, body, and spirit, for He is constantly listening to your prayers. Believe in Him, for He will never leave you nor forsake you. God bless you all.

He has showed you, O man, what is good. And what does the Lord require of you? To act justly and to love mercy and to walk humbly with your God. Micah 6:8

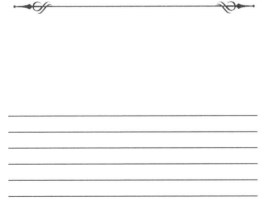

Today's Personal Message
August 2nd

My prayer for you today is to stop and
close your eyes, take time to enjoy the feelings
of being blessed by God's unconditional Love.
Let the waters of forgiveness wash over you
and receive His healing power.
God bless you.

"For I know the plans I have for you,"
declares the Lord, "plans to prosper you and
not harm you, plans to give you hope and a future,"
Jeremiah 29:11

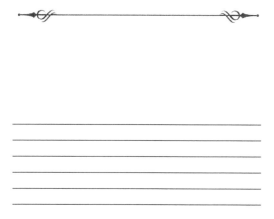

Today's Personal Message

August 3rd

*My prayer for you today is to not be afraid
to speak your mind but ask for God's
guidance before you speak.
God bless you.*

*Yet I am always with you; you hold me by my right
hand. You guide me with your counsel, and
afterward you will take me into glory. Whom have
I in heaven but you? And earth has nothing I desire
besides you. My flesh and my heart fail, but God is the
strength of my heart and my portion forever.
Psalm 73:23-26*

TODAY'S PERSONAL MESSAGE
August 4th

*My prayer for you today is one of compassion
and healing. Let yourself be surrounded by God's
Love and know that you are His child and He is
always holding you by His right hand.
God bless us all.*

*"The Lord bless you and keep you; the Lord makes
his face shine upon you and be gracious to you;
the Lord turns his face towards you
and give you peace."
Numbers 6:24-26*

Today's Personal Message
August 5th

My prayer for you today is to be still, sit in the Presence of God. Listen closely to His voice talking straight to you. Remember that He will always be listening to your prayers. Be still and feel His healing Presence and Love all around you.
God bless you.

But I am like an olive tree flourishing in the house of God; I trust in God's unfailing love forever and ever.
Psalm 52:8

TODAY'S PERSONAL MESSAGE
August 6th

*My prayer for you today is when you find
yourself in trouble, pray to the Lord our God and leave
your problems in his most capable hands.
Trust and believe in all the miracles He has waiting for
you. Receive them and be thankful for all His blessings.
God bless you.*

*Find rest, O my soul, in God alone; my hope
comes from him. He alone is my rock and
my salvation; he is my fortress.
I will not be shaken.
Psalm 62: 5-6*

TODAY'S PERSONAL MESSAGE
August 7th

My prayer for you today is to empty your mind with thoughts of knowing everything and stop trying to figure out ways to solve all your problems. Step into the Presence of God's loving salvation, and receive the real and true answer.
God bless you all.

But you are a chosen generation, a royal priesthood, a holy nation, His own special people, that you may proclaim the praises of Him who called you out of the darkness into His marvelous light.
Peter 2:9

TODAY'S PERSONAL MESSAGE
August 8th

*My prayer for you today is to never take the
privilege of knowing Jesus Christ as your Lord
and Savior for granted. Keep Him first and
foremost in your daily thoughts and be constant in
thanksgiving to Him for his many blessings.
God bless you.*

*"For my thoughts are not your thoughts, neither are your
ways my ways." declares the Lord. "As the heavens are
higher than the earth, so are my ways higher than your ways
and my thoughts than your thoughts."*
Isaiah 55:8-9

Today's Personal Message
August 9th

*My prayer for you today is to stop and
look at yourself as God sees you and know that He
created you in His own image. He is covering you always
with his robe of righteousness; He is always by your side.
God bless you.*

*Now to him who is able to do immeasurably
more than all we ask or imagine, according to
his power that is at work within us, to him be
glory in the church and in Christ Jesus.
Ephesians 3:20-21*

TODAY'S PERSONAL MESSAGE
August 10th

*My prayer for you today is to stay on the
right path even though sometimes it may be rocky
and dark. Trust in God to bring you back to center.
Know that He is always with you.
God bless you always.*

*Let the morning bring me word of your
unfailing love, for I have put my trust in you.
Show me the way I should go,
for you lift up my soul.
Psalm 143:8*

TODAY'S PERSONAL MESSAGE
August 11th

*My prayer for you today is to give of
yourself with all your heart to others around
you, as you give your love to God.
Listen to Him guide you and receive the
many blessings He has for you.
God bless you.*

*When Jesus spoke again to the people
he said, "I am the light of the world.
Whoever follows me will never walk in
darkness, but will have light of life."
John 8:12*

TODAY'S PERSONAL MESSAGE
August 12th

*My prayer for you today is to know
that He knows exactly what you need.
Trust in God's plan for you. Give thanks
for the many blessings He will place
upon you all your days.
God bless you.*

*So we fix our eyes not on what is seen,
but on what is unseen. For what is seen is
temporary, but what is unseen is eternal.
2 Corinthians 4:18*

_____
_____
_____
_____
_____
_____

TODAY'S PERSONAL MESSAGE
August 13th

My prayer for you today is to enjoy life,
enjoy each other, and enjoy God and his
wonderful Blessings. May God's healing hand
hold you up in all your needs.
God bless you all.

I have told you these things, so that in Me you may have
[perfect] peace and confidence. In the world you have
tribulation and trials and distress and frustration; but be
of good cheer For I have overcome the world.
[I have deprived it of power to harm you and have
conquered it for you.]
John 16:33

Today's Personal Message
August 14th

*My prayer for you today is that a Miraculous Healing
will come down upon you this very Moment, and may
God's mercy be in your heart, and in your soul, and in
your mind. Rest in His Presence and do not be afraid for
He is with you every step of the way.
God bless you.*

*I can do everything through him who
gives me strength.
Philippians 4:13*

TODAY'S PERSONAL MESSAGE
August 15th

*My prayer for you today is to see all God's
blessings in everything, even in the difficult times.
Trust Him always, for He will lead
you on to the right path.
God bless you.*

*Jesus answered, "I am the way and the
truth and the life. No one comes to
the Father except through me."
John 14:6*

TODAY'S PERSONAL MESSAGE
August 16th

My prayer for you today is to know that God has awakened in your heart. Love Him every minute every second of every day and His blessings will be with you always.
God bless you.

"You will seek me and find me when you seek me with all your heart."
Jeremiah 29:13

Today's Personal Message
August 17th

My prayer for you today is to know that
you belong to God, and you do not have to fear
anything. Trust in His healing power.
Pray for each other.
God bless you.

To him who is able to keep you from falling and
to present you before his glorious presence
without fault and with great joy—to the only God our
Savior be glory, majesty, power, and authority, through
Jesus Christ our Lord, before all ages, now and
forevermore! Amen.
Jude 24:25

Today's Personal Message

August 18th

*My prayer for you today is to know and
trust that God will be with you in all circumstances
and he will protect you always. Believe!
May God bless you always.*

*And you were included in Christ when you heard the
word of truth, the gospel of your salvation. Having
believed, you were marked in him with a seal, the
promised Holy Spirit, who is a deposit guaranteeing our
inheritance until the redemption of those who are God's
possession-to the praise of his glory.
Ephesians 1:13-14*

Today's Personal Message
August 19th

My prayer for you today is to draw close to
God and tell Him how much you need Him.
Our Father is always listening to your prayers.
God bless you.

My purpose is that they may be encouraged in
heart and united in love, so that they may have
the full riches of complete understanding, in order
that they may know the mastery of God, namely Christ,
in whom are hidden all the treasures of
wisdom and knowledge.
Colossians 2:2-3

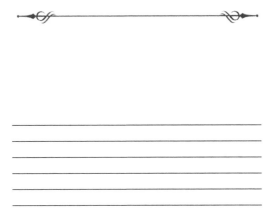

TODAY'S PERSONAL MESSAGE

August 20th

My prayer for you today is to ask God for His healing Presence to come to you and lift you up out of the pain and suffering of this failed world. Believe in His healing Power. Receive His awesome Love.
May God bless you.

"For I am the Lord your God, who takes hold of your right hand and says to you, Do not fear; I will help you."
Isaiah 41:13

Today's Personal Message

August 21st

*My prayer for you today is to stay on the path that God
has set before you, stay constant in prayer, and know that
He is the truth and the light of your life.
God bless you.*

*Be anxious for nothing, but in everything
by prayer and supplication with thanksgiving
let your request be known to God.
Philippians 4:6*

_____

_____

_____

_____

_____

_____

Today's Personal Message
August 22nd

*My prayer for you today is to trust
God with all your heart and soul, proclaim
His mighty Name when you are afraid,
and He will comfort you.
God bless you.*

*Look to the Lord and his strength;
seek his face always.*
Psalm 105:4

TODAY'S PERSONAL MESSAGE
August 23rd

*My prayer for you today is to love God
with all your heart and soul, give Him
everything you have and receive
all he has for you.
God bless you.*

*But he said to me, "My grace is sufficient for you,
for my power is made perfect in weakness."
Therefore I will boast more gladly about my
weaknesses, so that Christ's power may rest on me.
2 Corinthians 12:9*

TODAY'S PERSONAL MESSAGE

August 24th

*My prayer for you today is to know that God has
searched you and knows you and will always be
with you. Believe in Him, Love Him and search for his
healing forgiveness in His word.
God bless you*

*But as for me, I watch in hope for the
Lord, I wait for God my Savior;
my God will hear me.
Matthew 7:7*

———◦———————————————————◦———

_____
_____
_____
_____
_____
_____

Today's Personal Message
August 25th

My prayer for you today is to realize the
"I am" in your life. Proclaim it, shout it out
"I am". God is constantly blessing you and healing your
hurting Hearts, Minds, and Spirits. Proclaim it "I am".
God bless you.

I am always with you, to the very end of age."
Matthew 28:20

_____

_____

_____

_____

_____

_____

Today's Personal Message

August 26th

My prayer for you today is to ask God for His
forgiveness, and receive His blessing, and never
again be afraid of anything.
Remember that He loves you always.
God bless you.

"Who of you by worrying can add a single hour to his life?
Since you cannot do this very little thing, why do you
worry about the rest?"
Luke 12:25-26

Today's Personal Message
August 27th

My prayer for you today is to know that you will one day bear the fear of death and dying, but Jesus will walk hand and hand with you in this life and He will see you to the other side, open the gates and guide you into Heaven. All you have to do is trust, believe, and follow Him. Do not be afraid for God always has you by the right hand. God bless you all.

And do not grieve the Holy Spirit of God, with whom you were sealed for the day of redemption.
Ephesians 4:30

TODAY'S PERSONAL MESSAGE
August 28th

*My prayer for you today is to be a part of
something larger than yourself. Be a part of God's
Love and His Glory that dwells inside you! Stay
on the path He has placed before you and give Him
thanks every step of the way.
God bless you all.*

*In his heart a man plans his course,
but the Lord determines his steps.*
Proverbs 16:9

Today's Personal Message

August 29th

My prayer for you today is stop worrying about things.
Be quiet in His Presence. Know that God and the Holy
Spirit are guiding you through this life and
will never ever let you go.
God bless you.

"Do not let your heart be troubled. Trust in God; trust also
in me. In my Father's house are many rooms; if it were
not so, I would have told you. I am going there to prepare
a place for you."
John 14:1-2

Today's Personal Message

August 30th

My prayer for you today is to stay on the path that God has chosen for you, receive all His blessings, and give thanks for all His many gifts, and trust that His path is the right path for you.
God bless you.

The heavens declare the glory of God; the skies proclaim the work of his hands. Day after day they pour forth speech; night after night they display knowledge.
Psalm 19:1-2

TODAY'S PERSONAL MESSAGE
August 31st

My prayer for you today is to ask God for the strength to get you through this day. No matter what comes your way He will be by your side always.
God bless you.

Blessed are those who have learned to acclaim you, who walk in the light of your presence. O Lord.
Psalm 89:15

_____
_____
_____
_____
_____
_____

Today's Personal Message
September 1st

*My prayer for you today is know that every day with God
in your heart and His word on your lips is a Great Day.
He promised He will be watching over us always.
God bless you.*

*He will be the sure foundation for your times, a rich store
of salvation and wisdom and knowledge; the fear of the
lord is the key to this treasure.*
Isaiah 33:6

Today's Personal Message
September 2nd

*My prayer for you today is to seek out your own vision of
God's beautiful work in you. Know that He is right here
with you always, waiting to give you strength to live a
blessed life through Him.
God bless you.*

*And they were calling to one another: "Holy, holy, holy is
the Lord Almighty; the whole earth is full of his glory."
Isaiah 6:3*

Today's Personal Message

September 3rd

My prayer for you today is when you lose sight
of your faith and get confused about this life,
ask God quietly to help you get back on track. He
will lift you up higher than you could ever imagine.
God bless you.

Find rest, O my soul, in God alone;
my hope comes from him.
Psalm 62:5

TODAY'S PERSONAL MESSAGE

September 4th

*My prayer for you today is to always remember
to walk close to God our Father, for with Him
there is Light in this Life.
God bless you.*

*Humble yourselves, therefore, under God's
mighty hand, that He may lift
you up in due time.
1 Peter 5:6*

_____

_____

_____

_____

_____

_____

Today's Personal Message
September 5th

*My prayer for you today is to know that you have
had many friends that have passed through your life,
but the one true Friend that is with you then, now,
and will always be at your side is God the Father,
almighty Son and Savior of the world.
God bless you.*

*For it is God who works in you to will and
to act according to his good purpose.
Philippians 2:13*

Today's Personal Message
September 6th

My prayer for you today is to constantly seek
God's favor and forgiveness and receive His
many blessings that he has for you. He will
heal your broken life.
May God bless you.

Enter his gates with thanksgiving and his courts with
praise; give thanks to him and praise his name.
Psalm 100:4

_____
_____
_____
_____
_____
_____

TODAY'S PERSONAL MESSAGE
September 7th

*My prayer for you today is to know that when it
comes to serving the Lord our God there is no greater
Love that you will ever know. Amen?
God bless you.*

*So then, just as you received Christ
Jesus as Lord, continue to live in him, rooted and
built up in him, strengthened in the faith as you
were taught, and overflowing with thankfulness.*
Colossians 2:6-7

TODAY'S PERSONAL MESSAGE
September 8th

*My prayer for you today is for you to be
healed of all sickness! Then I ask for you to pray
for your own self to be healed and for the
healing of each other.
May God bless you.*

*Then Jesus came to them and said,
"All authority in heaven and on earth
has been given to me."
Matthew 28:18*

TODAY'S PERSONAL MESSAGE
September 9th

My prayer for you today is to always
Remember that no matter how far you roam
from God's path, just ask for His guidance
and He will set you straight again.
God bless you.

Taste and see that the Lord is good; blessed
is the man who takes refuge in him.
Psalm 34:8

_____

_____

_____

_____

_____

_____

TODAY'S PERSONAL MESSAGE
September 10th

My prayer for you today is to know that "you
belong to Jesus, and nothing can ever harm you"
Maudie Budde 1979
God bless you all.

She is clothed with strength and dignity;
she can laugh at the days to come.
Proverbs 31:25

Today's Personal Message
September 11th

My prayer for you today is to forget about your troubles for this moment and rejoice in the gift of knowing that God has you in the palm of His hand. Rejoice!
God bless you always.

You will keep him in perfect peace, whose mind is stayed on You, because he trust in You.
Isaiah 26:3

_____
_____
_____
_____
_____
_____

Today's Personal Message
September 12th

*My prayer for you today is to believe in the power
of God Almighty. Avoid the temptations of this world
for He will see you into the gates of Heaven and there
you will find His promise of Peace.
God bless you.*

*"The thief comes only to steal and kill and
destroy; I have come that they may have life,
and have it to the full."
John 10:10*

_____

_____

_____

_____

_____

_____

Today's Personal Message
September 13th

My prayer for you today is that you learn to not judge
yourself and others. Learn to Love yourself, everyone and
everything through the eyes of Jesus Christ. Amen
God bless you.

The Spirit of the Lord is on me, because he has
anointed me to preach good news to the poor. He
has sent me to proclaim freedom for the prisoners
and recovery of sight for the blind, to release the
oppressed and to proclaim the year of the Lord's favor.
Luke 4:1-19

TODAY'S PERSONAL MESSAGE
September 14th

*My prayer for you today is to stay close to God
all the days of your life. Walk with Him and
He will protect you always.
God bless you all.*

*Always giving thanks to God the Father for
everything, in the name of the Lord Jesus Christ.
Ephesians 5:20*

TODAY'S PERSONAL MESSAGE
September 15th

*My prayer for you today is for you to make time for
reflection today. Give of yourself to God our Father.
Thank Him for all the many blessings he has
waiting for you now and always.
May God bless you.*

*You will keep him in perfect peace, whose mind is
stayed on You, because he trust in You.
Isaiah 36:3*

_____
_____
_____
_____
_____
_____

TODAY'S PERSONAL MESSAGE

September 16th

*My prayer for you today is to be the best
you can be and ask the Holy Spirit to make
you the best He knows you are.
God bless you.*

*"Then you will know the truth, and the
truth will set you free."
John 8:32*

_____
_____
_____
_____
_____
_____

Today's Personal Message

September 17th

*My prayer for you today is to give yourself and
all your worries to God our Father and trust in His will
for you. Walk with Him, holding His right hand.
Let Him lead the way for you.
Believe in His Healing Power!
God bless you always!*

*I can do everything through him who
gives me strength.
Philippians 4:13*

_____
_____
_____
_____
_____
_____

TODAY'S PERSONAL MESSAGE
September 18th

*My prayer for you today is to be in tune
with the word of God and let His blessings guide
you in everything you do every day.
God bless you.*

*In the morning, O Lord, you hear my voice;
in the morning I lay my requests before you and
wait in expectation.*
Psalm 5:3

_____
_____
_____
_____
_____
_____

Today's Personal Message
September 19th

My prayer for you today is to ask God for his forgiveness and receive His unconditional Love, for with in His Spirit you will find the healing power you seek. God bless you.

A righteous man may have many troubles,
but the Lord delivers him from them all.
Psalm 34:19

_____

_____

_____

_____

_____

_____

Today's Personal Message
September 20th

*My prayer for you today is to know that
whatever troubles come your way, you are equipped
to overcome them with the help of God's healing
power and the Power of prayer.
God bless you.*

*"God is spirit, and his worshipers must
worship in spirit and in truth."
John 4:24*

Today's Personal Message

September 21st

My prayer for you today is to sit quietly and listen to God in your heart, telling you to stay constant in prayer and never give up hope. He knows your needs and hears your prayers! He will never give up on you. Ask and wait patiently in expectation.
God bless you.

Many are the plans in a man's heart, but it is the Lord's purpose that prevails.
Proverbs 19:21

TODAY'S PERSONAL MESSAGE

September 22nd

My prayer for you today is that when you wake up in
fear and are worried about life's troubles, turn your
thoughts to God our Father for His
strength and His song.
God bless you.

The spirit and the bride say, "Come!" And let him
who hears say, "Come!" Whoever is thirsty, let him
come; and whoever wishes, let him take the free
gift of the water of life.
Revelation 22:17

TODAY'S PERSONAL MESSAGE
September 23rd

My prayer for you today is to know that if you
Walk daily with God our Savior, all of your fears
Will be taken away and he will forgive all your
Sins and heal all your broken dreams.
God bless you all.

"All that the Father gives me will come to me, and
whoever comes to me I will never drive away."
John 6:37

_____
_____
_____
_____
_____
_____

Today's Personal Message
September 24th

My prayer for you today is to be of good cheer for God is with you all the days of your life. Ask and you shall receive the many blessings He has for you. God bless you.

In my integrity you uphold me and Set me in your presence forever.
Psalm 41:12

_____
_____
_____
_____
_____
_____

Today's Personal Message
September 25th

*My prayer for you today is to know that your
Paths are all different and unique, but also know
That you are all the same in the eyes of God. Receive
His one simple blessing for all your simple needs.
God bless you all.*

*When Jesus spoke again to the people, he said, "I am the
light of the world. Whoever follows me will never walk in
darkness, but will have the light of life."
John 8:12*

Today's Personal Message
September 26th

*My prayer for you today is for you to receive the
Word of God every second, every minute, with every
breath you take. Know that He is there for you.
Believe in His Power to save you.
God bless you.*

*But if from there you seek the Lord your God,
You will find him if you look for him with all your
Heart and with all your soul.
Deuteronomy 4:29*

TODAY'S PERSONAL MESSAGE
September 27th

*My prayer for you today is to rejoice in God's healing
blessings and receive all the gifts He has set aside for you.
Thank Him constantly for He is constantly
holding you by His mighty Right Hand.
God bless you.*

*The thief comes only to steal and kill and destroy;
I have come that they may have life, and have it to
the full. I am the good Shepherd. The good shepherd
lays down his life for his sheep."
John 10:10-11*

Today's Personal Message
September 28th

*My prayer for you today is to stay close to God's
mighty word. He will protect you and watch over you
all the days of your life. He will heal your pain.
God bless you.*

*Therefore he is able to save completely those
who come to God through him, because he
always lives to intercede for them.*
Hebrews 7:25

_____
_____
_____
_____
_____
_____

TODAY'S PERSONAL MESSAGE
September 29th

*My prayer for you today is to realize that God is
with you and in you at all times, trust that He
will never leave you alone.
God bless you.*

*"Though the mountains be shaken and the hills be
removed, yet my unfailing love for you will not be
shaken nor my covenant of peace be removed,"
says the Lord, who has compassion on you.
Isaiah 54:10*

TODAY'S PERSONAL MESSAGE
September 30th

My prayer for you today is to stop and take a
moment to be in God's Presence! Be bold and ask
Him for all the things you need, and then receive
them, with thanksgiving.
God bless you.

"Be still, and know that I am God;
I will be exalted among the nations,
I will be exalted in the earth."
Psalm 46:10

_____
_____
_____
_____
_____
_____

Today's Personal Message

October 1st

My prayer for you today is a simple prayer,
"Love yourself as God loves you."
May He bless you always.

O Lord, our Lord, how majestic is your name in all the
earth! You have set your glory above the heavens. From
the lips of children and infants you have ordained praise
because of your enemies, to silence the foe and the
avenger. When I consider your heavens, the work of your
fingers, the moon and the stars, which you have set in
place, what is man that you are mindful of him?
Psalm 8:1-4

Today's Personal Message
October 2nd

*My prayer for you today is to see yourself as
God sees you, forgive yourself as God forgives you.
Believe in yourself as God believes in you and
trust in God as He trust in you.
God bless you.*

*The Lord confides in those who fear him;
he makes his covenant known to them.
My eyes are ever on the Lord, for only he will
release my feet from the snare.
Psalm 25:14-15*

_____
_____
_____
_____
_____
_____

Today's Personal Message
October 3rd

*My prayer for you today is to trust in
God's plan for you, give into His will and
believe in His miracles coming your way.
God bless you.*

*Therefore, there is no condemnation for those
who are in Christ Jesus, because through Christ Jesus
the law of the Spirit of life set me free from the
law of sin and death.*
Romans 8:1-2

Today's Personal Message
October 4th

*My prayer for you today is to believe with
all your heart and soul that God is with you every
step of the way, and trust that His mighty word
will guide you safely through this life.
God bless you.*

*Don't you know that you yourselves are God's
temple and that God's Spirit lives in you?
1 Corinthians 3:16*

_____
_____
_____
_____
_____
_____

TODAY'S PERSONAL MESSAGE
October 5th

My prayer for you today is to sleep in the arms of our Savior today and all the days ahead of you. Trust in God's plan for you. Rejoice in this heavenly place that is yours. God bless you.

Surely God is my salvation; I will trust and not be afraid. The Lord, the Lord himself, is my strength and my song; he has become my salvation.
Isaiah 12:2

TODAY'S PERSONAL MESSAGE

October 6th

*My prayer for you today is for you to pray for
yourselves and for your loved ones.
God is always listening.
God bless you.*

*A righteous man may have many troubles,
but the Lord delivers him from them all.
Psalm 34:19*

_____

_____

_____

_____

_____

_____

Today's Personal Message

October 8th

My prayer for you today is to give all your worries to
God. Trust in His mighty power to heal you inside and out.
Love Him always for he always will love you.
God bless you.

Lean on, trust in, and be confident in the Lord
with all your heart and mind do not rely on
your own insight or understanding.
Proverbs 3:5

_____
_____
_____
_____
_____
_____

Today's Personal Message
October 8th

My prayer for you today is to repeat and understand the following words; "I am"! Now add your affirmations to the end. "I am the best I can be." "I am healed." God bless you.

God said to Moses, "I am who I am. This is what you are to say to the Israelites: I am has sent me to you."
Exodus 3:14

_____
_____
_____
_____
_____
_____

Today's Personal Message
October 9th

My prayer for you today is to continue to hold onto God's right hand and trust the path he has chosen for you. He will lead you to where you need to be. God bless you always.

O Lord, you have searched me and you know me. You know when I sit and when I rise; you perceive my thoughts from afar. You discern my going out and my lying down; you are familiar with all my ways. Before a word is on my tongue you know it completely, O Lord.
Psalm 139:1-4

Today's Personal Message
October 10th

My prayer for you today is when you wake up afraid of life and the world around you, close your eyes again and reach out to God our Father, for He alone can give you the peace that you seek. Amen!
God bless you all.

Many are asking, "Who can show any good?" Let the light of your face shine upon us, O Lord. You have filled my heart with greater joy than with their grain and new wine abound. I will lie down and sleep in peace, for you alone, O Lord, make me dwell in safety.
Psalm 4:6-8

TODAY'S PERSONAL MESSAGE
October 11th

My prayer for you is to receive the healing power
of God the almighty, for he is truly the beginning
and the end. He is the Savior of the world.
God bless you.

Don't you know that you yourselves are God's
temple and that God's Spirit lives in you?
1 Corinthians 3:16

_____
_____
_____
_____
_____
_____

TODAY'S PERSONAL MESSAGE
October 12th

*My prayer for you today is to practice your
faith every moment, believing in God's love for you,
never being afraid to ask Him for his healing
Power to come down upon you. Amen
God bless you.*

*Let us hold unswervingly to the hope we profess,
for he who promised is faithful.
Hebrews 10:23*

TODAY'S PERSONAL MESSAGE
October 13th

*My prayer for you today is to remember always
how much Christ loves you and what He has given
up for you to be forgiven. Receive God's
many gifts, and give thanks.
God bless you.*

*God made him who had no sin to be sin for us, so that in
him we might become the righteousness of God.
2 Corinthians*

_____
_____
_____
_____
_____
_____

TODAY'S PERSONAL MESSAGE

October 14th

*My prayer for you today is to believe in the
power of prayer and trust that whatever you
are going through is for a higher purpose. Just believe
and God will carry you through the pain.
God bless you all.*

*You are my hiding place; you will protect me from
trouble and surround me with songs of deliverance.
Psalm 32:7*

_____
_____
_____
_____
_____
_____

Today's Personal Message
October 15th

My prayer for you today seek out the Father and let Him help you find your way. Trust in God's blessings and give Him thanks for all His many gifts.
God bless you.

See, darkness covers the earth and thick darkness is over peoples, but the Lord rises upon you and his glory appears over you.
Isaiah 60:20

_____
_____
_____
_____
_____
_____

Today's Personal Message
October 16th

My prayer for you today is to find yourself
being that beacon of light that lifts up your friends
and family, and in return you will be lifted higher
than you have ever known.
God bless you all.

Look to the Lord and his strength;
seek his face always.
Psalm 105:4

Today's Personal Message
October 17th

*My prayer for you today is to always look to God for
the answers to your problems. Give Him thanks for
all moments of your life. Good things in you will
grow in all His blessings. Amen
God bless you.*

*Submit to God and be at peace with him;
in this way prosperity will come to you.
Job 22:23*

Today's Personal Message
October 18th

My prayer for you today is to always be your best and take steps of trust on this road of life for God will lead you to success.
God bless you.

Now to him who is able to do Immeasurably more than all we ask or imagine, according to his power that is at work within us.
Ephesians 3:20

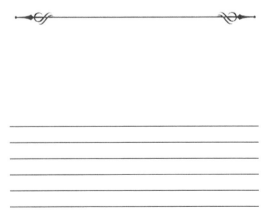

_____
_____
_____
_____
_____
_____

Today's Personal Message
October 19th

*My prayer for you today is to know
that God is the light, the truth and the way
to true happiness. Come to Him with open arms
and be born again out of the darkness into the Light.
God bless you all.*

*The city does not need the sun or the moon
to shine on it, for the glory of God gives it light,
and the Lamb is the lamp.
Revelation 21:23*

_____

_____

_____

_____

_____

_____

Today's Personal Message
October 20th

My prayer for you today is to be in tune with the precious word of our Lord God and Father. Listen to His voice inside of you and believe in His healing Presence. Amen God bless you all.

Therefore, as God's chosen people, holy and dearly loved, clothe yourselves with compassion, kindness, humility, gentleness and patience.
Colossians 3:12

TODAY'S PERSONAL MESSAGE

October 21st

*My prayer for you today is to cling to the right hand of
the Father and trust in his will. For you are children of
the all-powerful, all giving, and all loving God.
God bless you all.*

*Submit yourselves, then to God. Resist the
devil, and he will flee from you.
James 4:7*

Today's Personal Message

October 22nd

*My prayer for you today is to feel the Presence of God
in every step you take and every breath you breathe.
Proclaim His saving grace and be healed in the name
of His Son, Jesus Christ.
God bless you always.*

*But now in Christ Jesus you who once were far
away have been brought near through the
blood of Christ.
Ephesians 2:13*

_____
_____
_____
_____
_____
_____

Today's Personal Message

October 23rd

My prayer for you today is to not be afraid of any afflictions you may have, for God is holding you by His right hand, infusing you with His healing power. Believe in and receive this wonderful gift. God bless you.

The Lord replied, "My Presence will go with you, and I will give you rest."
Exodus 33:14

TODAY'S PERSONAL MESSAGE

October 24th

My prayer for you today is to slow down, close your eyes and visit with God in silence. Being in His Presence will bring you the peace that you so desire. God bless you all.

If the Lord delights in a man's ways, he makes his steps firm; though he stumbles, he will not fall, for the Lord upholds him with his hand.
Psalm 37:23-24

TODAY'S PERSONAL MESSAGE
October 25th

My prayer for you today is to stay constant in prayer
with God. Keep Him close by your side in all you do.
Always know that He is watching over you,
In Jesus name. Amen
God bless you.

In the same way, the Spirit helps us in our weakness.
We do not know what to pray for, but the Spirit himself
intercedes for us with groans that words cannot express.
Romans 8:26

Today's Personal Message

October 26th

*My prayer for you today is to see yourself as
a winner just as God sees you. Trust in His many
blessings for He will give you rest.
God bless you.*

*Come let us bow down in worship, let us kneel before the
Lord our Maker; for he is our God and we are the people of
his pasture, the flock under his care.*
Psalm 95:6-7

_____

_____

_____

_____

_____

_____

Today's Personal Message
October 27th

My prayer for you today is this. When you feel lost on your path, stop and simply ask God for directions, for He is the map that can set you straight and free. Trust in Him. He will never let you down.
God bless you.

But the fruit of the Spirit is love, joy, peace, patience, kindness, goodness, faithfulness.
Galatians 5:22

Today's Personal Message
October 28th

My prayer for you today is to forgive each other as you will be forgiven by God our Father and trust in His glorious plan for you.
For He will never let you go.
God bless you always.

"I am the Alpha and Omega," says the Lord God, "who is, and who was, and who is to come, the Almighty."
Revelation 1:8

TODAY'S PERSONAL MESSAGE
October 29th

*My prayer for you today is to feel the Presence of God our
Father with every breath you take. Keep Him in the
forefront of your every thought and dream and He will
always be present in every step of your journey.
God bless you.*

*Just as He chose us in Him before the foundation of the
world, that we would be holy and blameless before Him.
Ephesians 1:4*

TODAY'S PERSONAL MESSAGE
October 30th

*My prayer for you today is to know in your heart that
Jesus is with you always! For once you give yourself to
Him with all your heart, you belong to Him and nothing
can ever harm you from that moment on.
God bless you.*

*Show me your ways, O Lord; teach me your paths.
Psalm 25:4*

TODAY'S PERSONAL MESSAGE
October 31st

My prayer for you today is to listen to your inner voice which is God speaking to you, guiding you to know the Joy and Peace of the Holy Spirit. Trust and believe in this power that He has given you.
God bless you.

Through Jesus, therefore, let us continually offer to God a sacrifice of praise—the fruit of lips that confess his name.
Hebrews 13:15

TODAY'S PERSONAL MESSAGE
November 1st

My prayer for you today is to know in your most inner being that God's healing touch is surrounding you every moment of your life. Remember that God is always with you and He will help you find your way in the dark!
He is the Light.
God bless.

To shine on those living in darkness and in the shadow of death, to guide our feet into the path of peace.
Luke 1:79

TODAY'S PERSONAL MESSAGE
November 2nd

My prayer for you today is to love yourself as God loves
you. Give thanks to the Father for everything.
May God bless you and heal you.

Blessed are those who have learned to acclaim you, who
walk in the light of your presence, O Lord.
Psalm 89:15

_____

_____

_____

_____

_____

_____

Today's Personal Message
November 3rd

*My prayer for you today is for you to always believe in
the power of God, for He will truly set you free.
God bless you.*

*Which God will bring out in his own time-God,
the blessed and only Ruler, the King of kings and
Lord of lords, who is immortal and who lives in
unapproachable light, whom no one has seen or can see.
To him be honor and might forever. Amen.
1 Timothy 6:15-16*

TODAY'S PERSONAL MESSAGE

November 4th

*My prayer for you today is to quietly ask God
for his help and guidance and know that He will be
there with the answer and then just receive His
Healing Power and Glory.
God bless you.*

*"Ask and it will be given to you;
seek and you shall find."*
Matthew 7:7

_____
_____
_____
_____
_____
_____

Today's Personal Message

November 5th

My prayer for you today is to live your life in the light of God's many blessings. Trust Him in all your days and give Him thanks always. God bless you.

Come near to God and he will come near to you. Wash your hands, you sinners, and purify your hearts, you double-minded.
James 4:8

_____
_____
_____
_____
_____
_____

Today's Personal Message
November 6th

*My prayer for you today is for you to not seek
fame or fortune at the expense of not seeking the
Kingdom first. Listen to me. God is waiting to
give you everything, but you must first seek Him
with a true, open and honest heart.
God bless you.*

*So we fix our eyes not on what is seen,
but on what is unseen. For what is seen is temporary,
but what is unseen is eternal.
2 Corinthians 4:18*

Today's Personal Message
November 7th

*My prayer for you today is to seek the kingdom
of God in all that you do and lead others to follow
His precious word.
God bless you all.*

*"For I am the Lord, your God, who takes hold of your right
hand and says to you, Do not fear; I will help you."*
Isaiah 41:13

TODAY'S PERSONAL MESSAGE

November 8th

*My prayer for you today is to look back on all
the many gifts God has bestowed on you and know
that with Jesus holding you up. Remember
that the Best Is yet to come.
God bless you.*

*For it is by grace you have been saved, through
faith-and this not from yourselves, it is the gift of
God—not by works, so that no one can boast.
Ephesians 2:8-9*

TODAY'S PERSONAL MESSAGE
November 9th

My prayer for you today is to know this,
that worrying about your future is a waste of time,
for God the Father and glorious Healer is in control.
Stay constant in prayer, full of hope.
Praise His mighty Name! Giving thanks for
all His blessings.
God bless you all.

Look to the Lord and his strength;
seek his face always.
Psalm 105:4

Today's Personal Message
November 10th

My prayer for you is to look deep into your soul and find the power of Jesus Christ that dwells in you, for He will see you through any troubles. Praise his Holy Name. God bless you.

In the shelter of your presence you hide them from the intrigues of men; in your dwelling you keep them safe from accusing tongues.
Psalm 31:20

Today's Personal Message
November 11th

My prayer for you today is to remember, ask and you
shall receive, give and you will be given, love and you will
be loved. These are His promises that are yours to keep.
Trust in the Lord always.
God bless you.

Do not be slothful in zeal, be fervent in spirit, and serve
the Lord. Rejoice in hope, be patient in tribulation,
Be constant in prayer.
Romans 12:11-12

_____

_____

_____

_____

_____

_____

TODAY'S PERSONAL MESSAGE
November 12th

*My prayer for you today is to know with all your heart
and soul that God is with you in all ways. He is giving you
all the blessings you need in your life every day. So believe
and receive with open arms and know that He is a
generous God who believes in you too.
God bless you.*

*"I am the vine; you are the branches. If a man remains in
me and I in him, he will bear much fruit; apart from me
you can do nothing."*
John 15:5

Today's Personal Message
November 13th

My prayer for you today is to find the peace inside yourself, the gift that God has placed inside of you. Ask and you shall receive, and give thanks for all His many blessings.
God bless you.

A bruised reed he will not break, and a smoldering wick he will not snuff out. In faithfulness he will bring forth justice."
Isaiah 42:3

Today's Personal Message
November 14th

*My prayer for you today is to trust in the Love that is
Christ Jesus inside you, and be blessed for we are all
sinners saved by His Precious Word.
God bless you.*

*Trust in him at all times, O people; pour out your
hearts to him, for God But those who hope in the
Lord will renew their strength. They will soar on
wings like eagles; they will run and not grow weary,
they will walk and not be faint,
Isaiah 40:31*

Today's Personal Message
November 15th

*My prayer for you today is to always hold your head up
when you are lost and are feeling like the burden of the
world is upon your shoulders, remember, God is with you
always, and you are always with Him.
God bless you.*

*Therefore let everyone who is godly pray
to you while you may be found; surely when the
mighty waters rise, they will not reach him.
Psalm 32:6*

Today's Personal Message
November 16th

*My prayer for you today is to confess your sins and be
forgiven, for God is a forgiving God, and He will guide you
into the glory of his kingdom.
May God bless you.*

*For this God is our God forever and ever,
he will be our guide even to the end.
Psalm 48:14*

TODAY'S PERSONAL MESSAGE
November 17th

My prayer for you today is to seek the forgiveness of the Father and He will give you Peace. Love each other and remember each other in your prayers.
God bless you.

The spirit and the bride say, "Come!" And let him who hears say, "Come!" Whoever is thirsty, let him come; and whoever wishes, let him take the free gift of the Water of life.
Revelation 22:17

_____
_____
_____
_____
_____
_____

Today's Personal Message

November 18th

My prayer for you today is to lead by example,
giving God the glory and praise for all the
beautiful gifts He has given to you.
God bless you.

"Though the mountains be shaken and the hills be
removed, yet my unfailing love for you will not be shaken
nor my covenant of peace be removed," says the Lord, who
has compassion on you.
Isaiah 54:10

Today's Personal Message
November 19th

My prayer for you today is to stay close to Jesus in this life He has chosen just for you. Don't ever be afraid for He is walking with you every step of the way. Trust in Him and stay on the path before you.
God bless you.

He who dwells in the shelter of the Most High will rest in the shadows of the Almighty.
Psalm 91:1

TODAY'S PERSONAL MESSAGE
November 20th

My prayer for you today is to love God above all things,
thanking Him for this very life He has given you. Trust in
Him, for His way is the true and only way.
God bless you.

Let us come before him with thanksgiving
and extol him with music and song.
Psalm 95:2

Today's Personal Message

November 21st

*My prayer for you today is to keep your thanks
and praises to God in the forefront of your every
thought and joyfully receive all of His
glorious gifts with open arms.
God bless you.*

*After this I heard what sounded like a roar of a great
multitude in heaven shouting: "Hallelujah! Salvation and
glory and power belong to our God."
Revelation 19:1*

_____
_____
_____
_____
_____
_____

Today's Personal Message

November 22nd

My prayer for you today is to remain thankful
to God in all circumstances, knowing that He is in
complete control of your life and will always be
by your side. Remember, "Ask and you will receive"
"Give and you will be given"
God bless you always.

Look to the Lord and his strength;
seek his face always.
Psalm 105:4

———————————————————————

_____
_____
_____
_____
_____
_____

TODAY'S PERSONAL MESSAGE
November 23rd

*My prayer for you today is to see yourself as God
sees you, strong, beautiful, healthy and thankful
for His beautiful gift of life.
God bless you.*

*In the same way, the Spirit helps us in our weakness.
We do not know what to pray for, but the Spirit himself
intercedes for us with groans that words cannot express.
Romans 8:26*

TODAY'S PERSONAL MESSAGE
November 24th

*My prayer for you today is to learn to stay
in prayer constantly, for the answers sometimes
comes when you least expect them.
God bless you.*

*One thing that I ask of the Lord, this is what I seek:
that I may dwell in the house of the Lord all the
days of my life, to gaze upon the beauty of the
Lord and seek him in his temple.*
Psalm 27:4

Today's Personal Message
November 25th

*My prayer for you today is to find yourselves in His arms
every morning and remain there all the day, and when
you lie down to rest always remember to give Him thanks,
for God will cradle you in His arms always.
God bless you.*

*May the God of hope fill you with all joy and peace
as you trust in him, so that you may overflow with
hope by the power of the Holy Spirit.
Romans 15:13*

TODAY'S PERSONAL MESSAGE
November 26th

My prayer for you today is to ask for forgiveness
for the wrongs you have done and you will be forgiven.
Ask for your heart, mind, body, and spirit to be healed
and it will be done in the name of the Father,
the Son and the Holy Spirit.
God bless you.

"Without faith it is impossible to please Him, for he who
comes to God must believe that He is, and that He is a
rewarder of those who diligently seek Him."
Hebrews 11:6

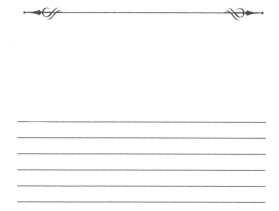

TODAY'S PERSONAL MESSAGE
November 27th

My prayer for you today is to stand fast in the word of the Lord, thanking Him for all His many blessings and give praise to His Holy Name.
God bless you.

Enter his gates with thanksgiving and his courts with praise; give thanks to him and praise his name.
Psalm 100:4

TODAY'S PERSONAL MESSAGE
November 28th

My prayer for you today is to know that inside
you is the blessings of our Lord. He provides you with
everything you need to succeed in every way in life.
Ask and you shall receive, give and it will be given to you.
Know that God's Love is in you already.
Just believe in Him in you.
God bless you.

Cast all your anxieties on him because
he cares for you.
1 Peter 5:7

TODAY'S PERSONAL MESSAGE

November 29th

*My prayer for you today is to know that when
you feel alone and afraid all you have to do is to say
"I belong to you Jesus" and be transformed in to the
miracle that He made you to be! Amen
God bless you.*

*"And whatsoever ye shall ask in my name, that
will I do, that the Father may be glorified in the Son.
If you shall ask anything in my name, I will do it."
John 14:13-14*

TODAY'S PERSONAL MESSAGE
November 30th

My prayer for you today is to stop worrying
about all your problems and give them to the
Father, for he holds you constantly in His hands.
Ask him to take your burdens, giving Him thanks and
then watch what happens!
May God bless you now and forever.

"God so loved the world that he gave his one and
Only Son, that whoever believes in him shall not
perish but have eternal life."
John 3:16

Today's Personal Message
December 1st

My prayer for you today is to learn to pray for yourself,
pray for your children and families, pray for our world,
and above all pray for each other. And listen quietly in
thanksgiving for God's answers.
God bless you.

The Lord appeared to us in the past, saying
"I have loved you with an everlasting love;
I have drawn you with loving-kindness."
Jeremiah 31:3

_____

_____

_____

_____

_____

_____

TODAY'S PERSONAL MESSAGE

December 2nd

*My prayer for you today is to be healed of
all your afflictions in the name of the Father and
the Son, and the Holy Spirit. Believe in the power
of God's mighty word and trust that He will deliver
you from your bonds.
May He bless you always and forever.*

*"Your words are trustworthy, and you
have promised these good things."*
2 Samuel 7:28

TODAY'S PERSONAL MESSAGE
December 3rd

My prayer for you today is to trust in His name "Jesus".
Be alive with Him inside you. Believe in His healing
power and His Love for you and the loved ones who you
love and pray for. Amen
God bless you. For God's Love is forever

"His compassions never fail.
They are new every morning."
Lamentations 3:22-23

_____
_____
_____
_____
_____
_____

TODAY'S PERSONAL MESSAGE

December 4th

My prayer for you today is that you are set free from the pain and sorrows of this world and are refreshed in the glory of God's loving arms. Trust in Him "Christ Jesus" and receive your miracle.
God bless you always.

Devote yourselves to prayer,
being watchful and thankful.
Colossians 4:2

Today's Personal Message
December 5th

My prayer for you today is to always be mindful of the
Presence of God around you, constantly acknowledging
His Power and His Peace in your heart.
Trust that He will take you where you need to go.
God bless you.

Let the peace of Christ rule in your
hearts.... And be thankful.
Colossians 3:15

Today's Personal Message

December 6th

*My prayer for you today is to love God our Father with
all your heart and soul, and receive all His glorious
blessings he has in store for you.
God bless you.*

*"Without faith it is impossible to please Him, for
he who comes to God must believe that He is,
and that He is a rewarder of those
who diligently seek Him."
Hebrews 11:6*

_____
_____
_____
_____
_____
_____

Today's Personal Message

December 7th

*My prayer for you today is to know that God our Father
is with you at all times. Trust that His healing power will
overcome all sickness and fear, and receive your Miracle.
God bless you.*

*May the God of hope fill you with all joy and peace
as you trust in him, so that you may overflow
with hope by the power of the Holy Spirit.
Romans 15:13*

TODAY'S PERSONAL MESSAGE
December 8th

*My prayer for you today is to rejoice in your
neediness and receive all the wonderful blessings that
He has in store for you.
God bless you.*

*And my God will meet all your needs according
to his glorious riches in Christ Jesus.
Philippians 4-19*

Today's Personal Message

December 9th

*My prayer for you today is to trust in God's
plan for you. Don't be afraid of the journey
up ahead, because He will keep you safe and
lead you right where you need to be.
God bless you.*

*"Whoever serves me must follow me; and
where I am, my servant will be. My Father will
honor the one who serves me. "
John 12:26*

_____

_____

_____

_____

_____

_____

Today's Personal Message
December 10th

My prayer for you today is to try to understand all people without judging them. Remember that your way is not the only way. Pray for each other and our country. Amen! God bless you.

Love the Lord your God with all you heart and with all you soul and with all your strength.
Deuteronomy 6:5

Today's Personal Message

December 11th

My prayer for you today is to constantly
live in His light. May God our Father bless you
and your dreams always.
God Bless you.

And my God will meet all your needs according
to his glorious riches in Christ Jesus.
Philippians 4-19

TODAY'S PERSONAL MESSAGE
December 12th

My prayer for you today is to know that Love,
that one and only Love that Jesus Christ has for you is
healing your heart and lifting you high. Remember,
He is always taking care of you.
God bless you.

"He holds victory in store for the upright".
Proverbs 2:7

TODAY'S PERSONAL MESSAGE
December 13th

*My prayer for you today is to practice being holy
in all that you do, and ask for God's forgiveness
for your short comings and receive His blessings.
God bless you.*

*Whatever you do, work at it with all your
heart, as working for the Lord, not for men.
Colossians 3:23*

_____
_____
_____
_____
_____
_____

Today's Personal Message

December 14th

My prayer for you today is to be happy and
place your worries and the worries of the world
in the hands of our Father God, constantly stay in
prayer for yourselves and for each other.
May God bless you.

So do not fear, for I am with you; do not be dismayed,
for I am your God. I will strengthen you and help you;
I will uphold you with my righteous right hand.
Isaiah 41:10

TODAY'S PERSONAL MESSAGE
December 15th

My prayer for you today is that you continually
ask for forgiveness, and that you never give up
Hope, for God is always listening.
God bless you all.

"Keep on asking and it will be given you;
keep on seeking and you will find; keep on
knocking and the door will be open to you."
Matthew 7:7

_____
_____
_____
_____
_____
_____

Today's Personal Message
December 16th

My prayer for you today is to be still in
His Presence, constant in prayer, patient in Hope,
for He has the answer waiting for you.
Believe and receive His glorious Miracles.
God bless you.

"Delight thyself also in the Lord; and he
shall give thee the desires of thine heart."
Psalm 37:4

TODAY'S PERSONAL MESSAGE
December 17th

My prayer for you today is to stay in the
Light of God's Love, receive all of His glorious gifts
and be thankful for all His many blessings.
May God our Father bless
and keep you on this Perfect day.

"Whoever serves me must follow me;
and where I am, my servant will be.
My Father will honor the one who serves me."
John 12:26

_____
_____
_____
_____
_____
_____

Today's Personal Message
December 18th

My prayer for you today is to listen to your inner voice.
That is God guiding you to where you need to go, He will
bless you in ways you cannot fathom. Give thanks and
praise to our Father for all that He does for you.
May God bless you.

"Be still, and know that I am God."
Psalm 46:10

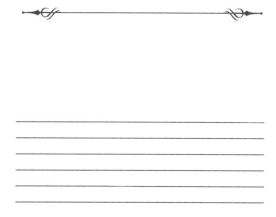

_____

_____

_____

_____

_____

_____

TODAY'S PERSONAL MESSAGE
December 19th

*My prayer for you today is to stay close to the Lord in
everything you do today and trust in His mighty Power
to bring the gifts of Heaven down to lift you up.
Believe in God's healing love for you. Amen.
God bless your every move.*

*In all ways acknowledge him, and
He will make your paths straight
Proverbs 3:6*

TODAY'S PERSONAL MESSAGE
December 20th

*My prayer for you today is to believe in His
miracles! Ask and you shall receive, give and
you will be given. Amen
May God bless you forever.*

*Pray that out of his glorious riches he may
strengthen you with power through his Spirit in
your inner being, so that Christ may dwell in
your hearts through faith.
Ephesians 3:16-17*

_____
_____
_____
_____
_____
_____

Today's Personal Message
December 21st

My prayer for you today is to expect your
Miracle, and receive it.
God bless you and keep you.

"I the Lord have called you in righteousness;
I will take hold of your hand. I will keep you
and will make you to be a covenant for the people
and a light for the Gentiles."
Isaiah 42:6

TODAY'S PERSONAL MESSAGE

December 22nd

*My prayer for you today is to trust in the Love
of God the Father, giving Him the glory for the
blessings in your life and always remember to
pray for yourself, your family and for each other.
May God our Father bless you in
these Holy Days!*

*Delight yourself in the Lord and he will
give you the desires of your heart.
Psalm 37:4*

_____
_____
_____
_____
_____
_____

TODAY'S PERSONAL MESSAGE
December 23rd

My prayer for you today is that you find your inner peace and love by knowing that Jesus Christ was born, lived, and died for you. Believe in His Love. Amen God bless you.

"I have come into the world as a light, so that no one who believes in me should stay in darkness."
John 12:46

Today's Personal Message

December 24th

My prayer for you today is to close your eyes,
bow your head and learn to pray to God our
Father with all your heart and soul. In silence
He will hear and answer you.
Amen. Let your prayers be heard in silence.
On this Merry Christmas Eve.
God bless you.

"Every good and perfect gift is from above."
James 1:17

TODAY'S PERSONAL MESSAGE
December 25th

*My prayer for you today is that you always remember
that our precious baby Jesus was born into this world to
lead you in to heaven by His life, death and resurrection.
Trust Him in all His plans for you.
Merry Christmas and God bless you all.*

*For God said, "Let light shine out of darkness," made his
light shine in our hearts to give us the light of the
knowledge of the glory of God in the face of Christ.
2 Corinthians 4:6*

―――――――――――――――――――――――

――――――――――――――――――――――――――
――――――――――――――――――――――――――
――――――――――――――――――――――――――
――――――――――――――――――――――――――
――――――――――――――――――――――――――
――――――――――――――――――――――――――

TODAY'S PERSONAL MESSAGE
December 26th

My prayer for you today is to know the Gift.
The Gift that is God is within you, for He is always
holding you close and will never let you go.
God bless you.

He who did not spare his own Son, but gave
him up for us all-how will he not also, along with
him, Graciously give us all things.
Romans 8:32

TODAY'S PERSONAL MESSAGE

December 27th

My prayer for you today is to walk in the light always remembering to pray for each other and yourselves, for prayer is the beginning of Healing. God bless you all today!

Trust him at all times, O people; pour out your hearts to him, for God is our refuge.
Psalm 62:8

_____

_____

_____

_____

_____

_____

TODAY'S PERSONAL MESSAGE
December 28th

My prayer for you today is to not be afraid
of anything, for God is with you always,
believing in you and watching over you and your
wellbeing! Open your eyes and your heart and receive
the many miracles God is performing in you.
God bless you.

Commit to the Lord whatever you do,
and your plans will succeed.
Proverbs 16:3

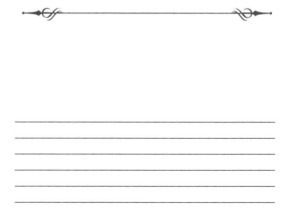

_____
_____
_____
_____
_____
_____

TODAY'S PERSONAL MESSAGE

December 29th

My prayer for you today is that you trust in
God with every fiber of your being!
And expect a miracle in your life.
God bless you.

Do you not know that your body is a temple of the Holy
Spirit, who is in you, whom you have received from God?
You are not on your own.
1 Corinthians 6:19

_____
_____
_____
_____
_____
_____

Today's Personal Message

December 30th

*My prayer for you today is to be willing
to let yourself be lead along God's Path.
Find yourself, and find yourself
loving each other.
May God our Father bless you.*

*"I am the vine; you are the branches.
If a man remains in me and I in him, he will
bear much fruit; apart from me
he can do nothing."*
John 15:5

Today's Personal Message
December 31st

My prayer for you today is to not be afraid,
but arise and rejoice in His Gift!
For He will take you places that you
never dreamed of.
Have a Blessed and Happy New Year.

When I am afraid I will trust in you. In God,
whose word I praise, in God I trust;
I will not be afraid.
What can mortal man do to me?
Psalm 56:3-4

TODAY'S PERSONAL MESSAGE

This is the last prayer of this devotional for the year.
It goes something like this. God bless you my friends.
Trust in the dreams and the vision that God has placed in
you. Be of good heart, constantly love yourself and each
other. Remember always that God our Father
is constantly healing your heart.
God bless you all.

Pray continually.
Thessalonians 5:17

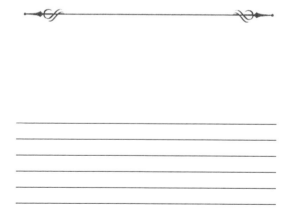

From the Author

These Daily Prayers are truly a gift from God; He just placed them in my Heart.

I thank The Holy Spirit every day for the many Gifts given me. God Bless You All!

Rusty Budde Bio

Rusty Budde grew up on a Horse Farm just outside of Houston Texas and has called Nashville TN. home for the past 33 years. Rusty credits the good Lord for blessing him with the gifts of being a Singer/Songwriter, and Record producer, and now a Christian book author. When God guided me toward praying for all my friends daily on Facebook everyone started to ask for more and more daily prayers. Now thousands of people following my daily post suggested the idea to do a book of daily prayers with a journal. So here it is. God bless you all!

CPSIA information can be obtained
at www.ICGtesting.com
Printed in the USA
LVHW031553100220
646431LV00001B/44